How to be a Great Boss

CRAFTED BY SKRIUWER

Copyright © 2024 by Skriuwer.

All rights reserved. No part of this book may be used or reproduced in any form whatsoever without written permission except in the case of brief quotations in critical articles or reviews.

For more information, contact : **kontakt@skriuwer.com** (www.skriuwer.com)

TABLE OF CONTENTS

CHAPTER 1: UNDERSTANDING THE TRUE MEANING OF LEADERSHIP

- Focus on leadership as service rather than power.
- Shift from personal ambition to moral accountability.
- Foster growth mindset, balancing authority with humanity.

CHAPTER 2: BUILDING TRUST AND CONFIDENCE

- Develop credibility through consistent words and actions.
- Use clear, honest communication to strengthen relationships.
- Establish fairness and accountability to create lasting trust.

CHAPTER 3: COMMUNICATING WITH CLARITY AND PURPOSE

- Craft messages to match both your intent and listener's needs.
- Combine logical structure with a genuine tone.
- Encourage two-way dialogue to prevent misunderstandings.

CHAPTER 4: SETTING GOALS THAT MOTIVATE TEAMS

- Align objectives with broader company vision.
- Balance ambition with achievable milestones.
- Reward progress and adapt goals to changing conditions.

CHAPTER 5: HANDLING CONFLICT & DISAGREEMENTS

- Identify root causes of friction early.
- Facilitate respectful dialogue and fair resolutions.
- Turn conflicts into growth opportunities for the team.

CHAPTER 6: FOSTERING A HEALTHY WORKPLACE CULTURE

- *Instill core values that guide daily behavior.*
- *Promote trust, mental well-being, and inclusion.*
- *Merge supportive policies with practical accountability.*

CHAPTER 7: TRAINING & DEVELOPING TEAM MEMBERS

- *Identify skill gaps and tailor learning plans.*
- *Blend on-the-job growth with formal coaching.*
- *Measure training outcomes for continuous improvement.*

CHAPTER 8: BALANCING AUTHORITY AND EMPATHY

- *Maintain firm leadership without losing compassion.*
- *Adapt your style to situations and individual needs.*
- *Foster mutual respect by listening, yet setting boundaries.*

CHAPTER 9: AVOIDING COMMON MANAGEMENT MISTAKES

- *Stay aware of pitfalls like micromanagement or vague goals.*
- *Offer timely, constructive feedback to avert bigger issues.*
- *Use consistent policies and fair decision-making processes.*

CHAPTER 10: LEADING THROUGH CHANGE

- *Clarify the vision behind new initiatives.*
- *Communicate openly and handle resistance tactfully.*
- *Provide resources and support for smooth transitions.*

CHAPTER 11: MEASURING PERFORMANCE AND GIVING FEEDBACK

- *Select relevant metrics tied to strategic aims.*
- *Deliver timely, specific, and balanced feedback.*
- *Use data without ignoring qualitative insights or morale.*

CHAPTER 12: ENCOURAGING PERSONAL ACCOUNTABILITY

- *Set clear roles so each person owns outcomes.*
- *Champion honesty and proactive problem-solving.*
- *Recognize self-driven behavior and learning from mistakes.*

CHAPTER 13: GROWING LONG-TERM BUSINESS RELATIONSHIPS

- *Build trust with clients, suppliers, and industry peers.*
- *Use transparent communication and fair negotiations.*
- *Maintain genuine interest in partners' challenges and goals.*

CHAPTER 14: MOTIVATING THROUGH REWARDS AND RECOGNITION

- *Acknowledge achievements with sincerity and depth.*
- *Tie recognition to core values and desired outcomes.*
- *Avoid superficial prizes; balance individual and team praise.*

CHAPTER 15: HANDLING STRESS AND BURNOUT

- *Recognize early signs of chronic pressure and fatigue.*
- *Introduce practical coping strategies and workload balance.*
- *Support mental health openly to sustain long-term well-being.*

CHAPTER 16: INSPIRING INNOVATION AND CREATIVITY

- *Encourage idea-sharing and safe-to-fail experiments.*
- *Combine structured methods with open-ended brainstorming.*
- *Reward problem-solving and cross-functional collaboration.*

CHAPTER 17: DECISION-MAKING TECHNIQUES FOR LEADERS

- *Blend rational analysis with informed intuition.*
- *Use tools like cost-benefit analysis and scenario planning.*
- *Communicate decisions transparently and review outcomes.*

CHAPTER 18: MANAGING DIFFERENT PERSONALITIES AND WORK STYLES

- *Adapt communication to introverts, extroverts, and varied traits.*
- *Balance structured vs. flexible approaches in tasks.*
- *Turn diversity in perspectives into a unifying strength.*

CHAPTER 19: BUILDING A LEGACY OF STRONG LEADERSHIP

- *Shape a sustainable culture and develop future leaders.*
- *Document processes, share knowledge, and avoid over-reliance on one person.*
- *Embed ethical, long-lasting practices that outlive your tenure.*

CHAPTER 20: PREPARING FOR THE FUTURE OF LEADERSHIP

- *Embrace new technologies and global team dynamics.*
- *Invest in upskilling, adaptability, and inclusive policies.*
- *Balance proven fundamentals with evolving workforce needs.*

Chapter 1: Understanding the True Meaning of Leadership

Being a boss can sound straightforward. You get a position of responsibility, give instructions, sign documents, and watch as your team carries out tasks. But real leadership goes beyond sending orders or waiting for results. It is a role that involves moral responsibility, social awareness, and personal growth. This chapter will look at what genuine leadership means, how it differs from power, and how it shapes the environment at work. These insights will extend beyond general advice and present information that is not widely known, offering a deeper look at the factors that make bosses effective and respected.

1.1 Shifting from Power to Service

A common misconception is that a boss holds power over others, but an effective leader focuses on serving rather than controlling. In many successful organizations, those at the top see their roles as helping staff thrive. Instead of ruling with fear or intimidation, these leaders aim to create an environment where people feel valued and supported. This helps foster loyalty and a sense of belonging among the workforce.

To serve effectively, a boss might:

- Provide resources that help teams function better, such as proper tools, clear guidelines, or relevant training sessions.
- Make sure there are no obstacles that hinder productivity and success.
- Show consistent concern for team members' overall well-being.

Shifting from a power-oriented mindset to a service-oriented one not only improves morale but also leads to better results because workers feel confident and supported. This approach encourages autonomy, which often sparks creativity and thorough thinking. Staff members who believe their boss cares about their success are more likely to share ideas and support one another.

1.2 The Boss as a Moral Compass

In any team, the boss sets the tone for ethics and morality. Actions, not just words, reflect these values. For example, if you say the company forbids shortcuts that compromise quality, but you allow such shortcuts to pass when deadlines loom, you risk losing the trust of your employees. On the other hand, if you consistently uphold high standards, even when it is hard, you let people see that honest leadership is alive within the team.

Real-life scenario: A manager in a software company needed to meet a very strict project timeline. The client demanded a certain feature, but the team realized a potential flaw in the code that could harm data security if not fixed properly. Instead of ignoring the flaw to meet the deadline, the manager decided to extend the timeline slightly, ensuring the team could address the issue thoroughly. Although it was a stressful choice, the boss's refusal to compromise on safety won respect. Eventually, the client recognized the company's integrity, leading to more partnerships.

Acting as a moral compass can show up in daily interactions:

- Being transparent about project hurdles.
- Responding fairly when conflicts occur.
- Holding people accountable for meeting standards in a way that fosters growth and skill improvement.

Over time, these regular examples of honesty build a culture where individuals see quality and ethics as crucial parts of their work.

1.3 Why Great Bosses Focus on Personal Growth

When someone is promoted to a leadership role, they might think they have "arrived." In reality, good leadership demands constant growth. Leading a group of individuals with diverse backgrounds means you must expand your perspectives, adapt your approaches, and stay aware of changing trends within your industry.

Practical Ways to Pursue Growth as a Boss

1. **Read Outside Your Usual Interests**: Explore books on behavioral psychology, problem-solving, and other areas that can sharpen your leadership skills.
2. **Connect with Experts**: Seek people in different fields who have faced challenges similar to yours. By learning from them, you discover alternative approaches.
3. **Test New Management Styles**: Once in a while, adjust your strategy. For instance, if you usually follow up on tasks daily, consider shifting to a more independent approach where employees provide updates only when needed. Observe the results and learn from them.
4. **Accept Constructive Criticism**: Even if it feels uncomfortable, well-intentioned feedback helps you find personal blind spots.

By dedicating time to personal development, you show employees that growth is a lifelong process. This attitude can trickle down, encouraging others to seek self-improvement.

1.4 Balancing Authority with Humanity

A boss must instruct and guide, but too much authority can intimidate. On the other hand, a lack of authority can cause chaos. The key is balancing authority with a human touch. You can be firm and clear about goals, deadlines, and standards, while still understanding the challenges your team faces.

Strategies to Maintain This Balance

- **Use Authority as a Tool, Not a Weapon**: Authority is there to keep processes on track, not to feed personal power.
- **Stay Attuned to Emotional Signals**: Watch for stress or frustration among your staff. Address these issues calmly and offer help. Sometimes a simple conversation can unravel hidden problems.
- **Model the Right Behavior**: If you want your team to be on time, show consistency in your own schedule. If you want them to take ownership, demonstrate that you also take ownership of your mistakes.

Practicing kindness doesn't mean you are weak. It means you can earn respect without threatening people. Clear guidelines, fair policies, and empathy can live together in harmony.

1.5 The Role of Long-Term Vision

Many bosses get lost in day-to-day tasks. True leadership, however, requires having a long-term plan that shapes decisions. If you understand your end goal, you can better align short-term tasks with that bigger picture. This clarity helps avoid random actions and sets purposeful steps toward growth.

Creating a Strong Vision

1. **Define the Future State**: Identify where you want the team or company to be in a few years. Be specific about size, market position, or the new capabilities you want.
2. **Share It Wisely**: While crafting the vision, get input from those who will help carry it out. This makes the vision more practical and gets people's support.
3. **Keep It Visible**: Write it down or discuss it regularly. People often forget if the vision is not reinforced.
4. **Adapt When Needed**: A good vision should be firm in its purpose but flexible in its methods, allowing you to handle unexpected changes.

Leaders who only think about immediate tasks can lose out on bigger opportunities. By keeping long-term vision in mind, you guide decisions in a logical direction, ensuring daily efforts contribute to lasting growth.

1.6 Hidden Factors That Build Leadership Strength

Besides the standard guidance like "listen to your team" or "communicate well," a few less-discussed factors can heighten a boss's influence:

1. **Consistency in Follow-Through**: If you promise feedback, give it. If you set a meeting, show up on time. Reliability makes people trust you.
2. **Strategic Simplicity**: Complicated projects can overwhelm teams. Trying to make things simpler, without reducing their core value, can help everyone stay focused.
3. **Skilled Delegation**: The best bosses are not those who do everything themselves, but those who know exactly what tasks they should assign to others. Delegating effectively frees you to concentrate on bigger issues and helps your team members grow.

4. **Self-Control in Stressful Moments**: A composed leader in tough times helps the entire team remain calm. Show people you can handle pressure without losing control. This sets an important example for others.

When these elements come together, they create a solid platform for you to be respected, not just obeyed.

1.7 Using Honest Self-Assessment

Another key to understanding leadership is reflecting on your own performance regularly. All bosses have blind spots. By spotting and addressing them, you stay in line with the principles of good leadership. Waiting for performance reviews or major failures can be risky. Instead, schedule times (perhaps once a month) to ask yourself questions like:

- "Did I communicate clearly with everyone on the team?"
- "Did I address any conflicts or did I ignore them?"
- "Have I recognized and encouraged any person who performed beyond expectations?"
- "Am I following my own guidelines, or have I slipped into bad habits?"

Being open to confronting your own shortcomings is what keeps you from drifting away from being a people-centered leader. This ongoing self-check helps you make small changes early, instead of facing big problems later.

1.8 Realizing Leadership Is a Responsibility, Not a Prize

Many people see management roles as trophies for personal ambition, but it is actually a job of constant accountability. You are responsible for the morale, well-being, and productivity of your staff. Their professional growth depends in part on how you guide them. Recognizing this may be sobering, but it also underscores the importance of doing it correctly.

Examples of Responsible Leadership

- **Upholding Team Morale**: When the team's mood is down, the boss should investigate the causes and find realistic ways to fix the problems.

- **Protecting Staff from Unfair Conditions**: If upper management or clients ask for the impossible, it is your job to shield your team or negotiate better terms.
- **Providing Resources**: If you notice employees struggling with outdated tools or software, act to secure modern resources that help them do their jobs well.

Leaders who view their role as a chance to serve and defend their teams gain long-term respect. This approach also stops high turnover, saving the company from constant recruitment and training costs.

1.9 Reasons Some Leaders Fail

Not every boss meets these expectations. Some take shortcuts or let power go to their heads. Common failure points include:

- **Ignoring Feedback**: Overconfidence leads them to dismiss ideas from the team.
- **Inconsistent Policies**: Changing rules according to mood causes confusion.
- **Lack of Empathy**: Treating people as replaceable rather than valuing their input.
- **Poor Time Management**: Unable to prioritize, they create stressful conditions for everyone.

Being aware of these hazards can help you avoid them. The best approach is to stay humble, keep learning, and pay attention to warning signs. Periodically check if you show any of these behaviors and correct them immediately.

1.10 Conclusion of Chapter 1

True leadership goes well beyond the idea of commanding. It requires a shift in mindset from power to service, maintaining ethical standards, setting clear visions, and cultivating an environment of trust and personal growth. By internalizing these values, you establish a solid foundation for effective guidance that helps not just the organization, but also the individuals under your management.

Chapter 2: Building Trust and Confidence

Trust and confidence form the core of strong leadership. Without trust, people may follow directions because they must, but not because they believe in the vision or feel genuinely committed to the boss's goals. Without confidence, a leader's capacity to guide effectively is undercut by hesitation or uncertainty. In this chapter, we will explore lesser-known practices and specific strategies to build trust and confidence in leadership roles, ensuring that these traits are solidly grounded in reality rather than empty statements.

2.1 Defining Trust and Confidence

While many use these terms loosely, it helps to define them more clearly:

- **Trust**: The belief that you will act with integrity, fairness, and consistency. People trust you when they see you regularly keeping your promises and valuing honesty even in difficult situations.
- **Confidence**: The certainty that you possess the skills, knowledge, or judgment to lead successfully. Confidence is shown by decisive actions, the willingness to be accountable, and the ability to remain calm when problems arise.

These qualities overlap. For instance, a confident boss appears more trustworthy because they manage stressful events without making irrational choices. Meanwhile, trust boosts a leader's confidence by ensuring the team will support and follow guidance.

2.2 Laying the Foundation for Trust

a) Consistency of Word and Action

It is vital for your team to see that your actions match your stated values and objectives. If you claim to value punctuality, consistently start meetings on time. If you talk about honesty, be transparent about challenges instead of hiding them. Such alignment between word and deed is often rare in some work environments, but those who practice it stand out as credible.

b) Fairness in Decision-Making

When decisions seem fair, people are more likely to trust leadership. Fairness doesn't always mean everyone gets what they want, but it means the process is clear and unbiased. Factors that boost fairness include:

- Explaining the reasoning behind decisions.
- Applying the same rules to everyone, regardless of personal relationships or office politics.
- Allowing team members to voice opinions and concerns before deciding.

c) Demonstrating Personal Responsibility

When mistakes occur, a trustworthy boss takes ownership. Blaming the team or external factors erodes trust quickly. Instead, acknowledging "I made a mistake" can actually raise a leader's standing because it shows maturity and honesty. Once you take responsibility, you can work on improvements without pointing fingers.

2.3 Practical Ways to Earn Trust

1. **Open-Door Sessions**: Schedule weekly or monthly time slots when anyone can speak with you privately. This helps staff see that you are genuinely open to their insights or concerns.
2. **Regular Updates**: Don't make people guess what's happening. Send out brief updates on ongoing projects, policy changes, or new company directions. This reduces rumors and fosters clarity.
3. **Transparent Reward Systems**: Make sure promotions and rewards follow clear guidelines. If people see that these are based on friendships or favoritism, trust is destroyed.
4. **Mindful Language**: The way you talk can hurt or help your reputation. Avoid making promises you can't keep. Use clear, direct language to prevent misunderstandings.

2.4 Strengthening Confidence as a Boss

Confidence isn't just about speaking loudly or dressing well, though those factors can affect first impressions. Real confidence stems from a collection of skills, experiences, and beliefs that you hold about your ability to deal with challenges.

a) Deep Knowledge of Your Field

One of the greatest paths to confidence is knowing your field thoroughly. This doesn't mean you must be the absolute best at every task your department handles, but you should have a broad understanding of key components. For instance, if you oversee a software development team, you should have a grasp of coding practices, testing methods, and project management strategies. This knowledge lets you ask better questions, understand suggestions from your staff, and form a realistic view of how projects advance.

b) Strategic Risk Management

Confident leaders are not reckless. Instead, they gauge potential outcomes and prepare contingency plans. This method balances the need for progress with an awareness of possible dangers. By ensuring that each decision is well-considered, you show the team that you are steering them with logic and thoughtful planning, not rushing into random actions.

c) Controlling Fear and Doubt

Even the most knowledgeable leaders face uncertainty. The difference is how they handle it. Instead of letting doubt undermine their authority, confident bosses accept that some unknowns exist but rely on proven processes, teamwork, and research to reduce risks. If something is unclear, they gather input from trusted experts or relevant data sources.

2.5 Linking Trust and Confidence in Daily Leadership

The real power comes when trust and confidence feed off each other. A boss with confidence in their decisions carries themselves in a way that the team recognizes as steady. When the team sees consistent follow-through and a respectful attitude toward their concerns, they trust the leader. This trust then bolsters the leader's confidence because they know the group will stand behind them.

Example Scenario

A product manager, newly appointed, has to lead a cross-functional team spread across multiple locations. She starts by holding one-on-one sessions with key members, learning about existing challenges, and clarifying each person's role. She shares her plan openly and asks for input on how to improve it. Initially, people are cautious, but seeing that she respects their time and knowledge, they begin to trust her. Because of this trust, the product manager feels confident in making tough decisions and adjusting timelines when necessary. Over time, the team works better together, achieving targets more smoothly than before.

2.6 Avoiding Behaviors That Undermine Trust and Confidence

A single poor choice can damage trust that took months or years to build. Some habits that weaken both trust and confidence include:

1. **Making Empty Promises**: When you tell a team member you will do something and fail to deliver, they lose respect for your word.
2. **Responding Aggressively to Feedback**: If people fear backlash for offering genuine insights, they will stop communicating issues.
3. **Shifting Blame**: Consistently blaming subordinates or outside conditions for failures signals to others that you can't manage adversity.
4. **Inconsistent Behavior**: Sudden changes in mood or direction can create confusion, suggesting a lack of well-thought-out strategy.

2.7 Little-Known Tools for Building Trust and Confidence

a) Field Visits and Shadowing

If your organization has multiple sites or departments, spend time working alongside frontline employees. This is sometimes overlooked by leaders who stay in offices and rely on second-hand reports. Field visits give first-hand knowledge and show your willingness to understand day-to-day realities.

b) 360-Degree Leadership Reviews

Many workplaces only conduct top-down assessments. Instead, set up a system where team members, peers, and even external partners can anonymously provide feedback about your leadership. Review these insights, share your reflections, and outline steps you plan to take for self-improvement. This method can be scary, but it communicates that you value honesty and growth.

c) Knowledge-Sharing Sessions

Organize regular sessions where team members, including you, share insights on new tools, industry changes, or best practices. By engaging actively, you show you are also a learner. This levels the hierarchy a bit and reinforces trust and respect.

2.8 The Power of Encouraging Independent Thinking

A leader who encourages employees to think independently shows both trust in them and confidence in the team's abilities. This can be achieved by:

- Giving them space to plan and manage smaller projects independently.
- Inviting fresh ideas on existing problems.
- Praising sensible risk-taking and not punishing mistakes made in good faith.

When you show trust in the team's capabilities, they often respond by producing more creative and effective solutions. This approach might lead to methods you wouldn't have considered on your own, driving innovation and saving time.

2.9 Handling Problems with Credibility

Crises and unexpected problems test the strength of trust and confidence. If an issue arises—a data breach, a product failure, or a public relations incident—team members look to the boss for guidance. How you respond sets an example:

- **Acknowledge the Issue**: Don't ignore it. Let people know you are aware of the problem.
- **Gather Facts Quickly**: Confirm the details, gather relevant data, and speak with those involved.
- **Keep People Updated**: People fear the unknown. Even if you don't have all the answers, periodic updates reduce speculation.
- **Act Decisively**: Once you have enough information, select a path forward and communicate it clearly.

A calm, fact-based response will strengthen trust in your leadership. This doesn't mean hiding the seriousness of the matter. Instead, it means being open about it while offering a well-thought-out action plan.

2.10 Building Trust and Confidence Over Time

Establishing trust and confidence is an ongoing process, not a one-time checkmark. You earn it gradually, through day-to-day interactions and decisions.

Practical Routine Strategies

- **Daily Huddles**: Short team meetings to share priorities, updates, and quick problem-solving. They show your involvement and keep everyone aligned.
- **Weekly or Biweekly Reviews**: More in-depth discussions to look back on achievements, address challenges, and highlight improvements for the next period.
- **Monthly One-on-Ones**: Time for each individual to talk about personal goals, concerns, or ideas. This setting encourages honest communication without distractions.
- **Quarterly Reflection**: Look at the bigger picture. Review team morale, project timelines, financial results, or any other key metrics. Share successes and learning points.

By remaining consistent in these activities, you build a pattern of trustworthiness. People see that you are attentive and that your confidence comes from staying informed.

2.11 The Link Between Trust, Confidence, and Team Wellness

Team wellness refers to the physical, mental, and emotional health of employees. When people trust their boss, they are more comfortable discussing workload issues, stress, and other challenges. Similarly, a confident leader can proactively set guidelines that keep workloads manageable and encourage healthy habits in the workplace.

Encouraging Wellness

- **Reasonable Work Schedules**: Make sure deadlines are realistic. Overloading employees repeatedly leads to fatigue, mistakes, and burnout.
- **Support Systems**: Consider offering mental health resources or flexible work arrangements.
- **Modeling Healthy Behavior**: If you want your team to stay balanced, avoid sending emails late at night or urging constant overtime.

Looking after the wellness of the team is both an ethical and a strategic choice. Healthy employees work at a higher level, and they feel valued when their well-being is respected.

2.12 Conclusion of Chapter 2

Trust and confidence act as the anchor for any high-functioning team. You build them gradually, through consistent actions, open communication, fair processes, and genuine concern for others. A leader who invests in these qualities will notice better morale, greater creativity, and fewer conflicts. These outcomes do not happen by chance; they are the result of deliberate efforts to practice authentic leadership.

The next chapters will explore further areas such as communication styles, setting motivating goals, and handling conflict in a productive way. All these topics connect with the themes of trust and confidence, since they shape how team members perceive their boss's intentions. By focusing on trust and confidence, you set a strong platform for every other skill and strategy you apply in the workplace.

Chapter 3: Communicating with Clarity and Purpose

When a leader's words are muddled or uncertain, even the strongest ideas can go astray. Effective communication is the art of conveying facts, goals, and strategies in a way that makes people take notice and want to act. As a boss, your ability to communicate well can mean the difference between a high-functioning team and one that struggles with misunderstandings. This chapter will explore hidden methods, practical examples, and useful tips for mastering clear, purposeful communication that keeps your team confident and informed.

3.1 Defining Clear Communication

Clear communication means that messages come across in a manner that matches your intent. It also means that listeners understand exactly what is expected of them. You might think this is obvious, but in reality, many workplace conversations lack clarity:

1. **Vague Language**: Leaders sometimes use phrases like "We need to do better" or "Let's step up our efforts" without explaining what that looks like.
2. **Conflicting Messages**: When one announcement promises a relaxed policy and another tightens requirements, confusion grows.
3. **Too Many Layers**: Overuse of buzzwords or unnecessary details can hide the main message.

When communication is unclear, staff can feel lost, uncertain, and less motivated. By focusing on specifics and avoiding extra fluff, you stand a better chance of building an environment where people know exactly what they need to do.

3.2 Why Purpose Matters

Communication is not only about the words you choose, but also about the "why" behind them. If you do not have a clear purpose, your words may just create noise. Purposeful communication ties what you say to a larger objective or plan. This helps people see the logic behind your requests or instructions.

For instance, consider a scenario where you ask your team to adopt a new software tool. Without purpose, you might say, "Let's start using this new tool from Monday." On the other hand, purposeful communication might be: "Starting Monday, we will switch to the new software to reduce manual data entry by 40% and improve our project tracking. This helps us handle our growing workload more efficiently."

The second message offers a reason for the change, making it easier for staff to see why it's worth their time and effort.

3.3 Hidden Pitfalls in Workplace Communication

Several communication pitfalls can appear in day-to-day operations:

1. **Assumed Knowledge**: A leader assumes employees already know the background of a project or a company policy. As a result, new or less-experienced employees feel lost.
2. **Emotional Leakage**: Leaders under stress sometimes let frustration slip into their statements, leading to short, abrupt remarks or angry outbursts.
3. **Closed Communication Loops**: This occurs when top executives discuss changes among themselves but do not clearly communicate them to all levels of the organization. Lower-level employees then feel blindsided when a new directive pops up.
4. **Distractions in Digital Channels**: With multiple emails, group chats, and project management tools, important messages can vanish among many less-important notifications.

Being aware of these hidden obstacles lets you create more careful, deliberate communication plans.

3.4 Channels of Communication and Their Impact

In today's workplace, communication can occur in many forms: face-to-face talks, email threads, chat apps, phone calls, and video conferences. Each channel has its pros and cons, and choosing the correct one is a leadership skill in itself.

1. **Face-to-Face Meetings**: Best for detailed discussions, performance reviews, or when delivering important news. You can note body language, ask clarifying questions, and build personal rapport.
2. **Emails**: Useful for sharing documented instructions, meeting summaries, and official information. However, emails can be misread if not worded properly. Overly long emails often lose the reader's attention.
3. **Instant Messaging Apps**: Good for quick updates or real-time collaboration, but can cause interruptions if used excessively. It also risks being less formal, so clarity can suffer.
4. **Video Conferences**: Helpful for remote teams. Video allows participants to see facial expressions, which can reduce misunderstandings. But technical glitches, connection problems, and scheduling across time zones can complicate them.
5. **Project Management Platforms**: Provide shared visibility of tasks and timelines. People can refer back to this information anytime, reducing confusion about roles and responsibilities.

An effective boss carefully chooses the channel that best fits the content and urgency of the message.

3.5 Methods to Increase Clarity

Communicating with clarity is an ongoing task that requires practice. Here are some methods that go beyond the usual suggestions:

1. **Align with Key Goals**: Before sending any message, ask yourself: "How does this connect to our broader objectives?" If it doesn't, consider whether the message is necessary or if it should be rephrased to connect with current aims.
2. **Layered Summary Technique**: When explaining a complex idea, begin with a brief overview that states the main points, then break them down step-by-step. Finish with a short recap so people can recall the key points easily.
3. **Periodic Pulse Checks**: After you share instructions or announcements, ask one or two team members to restate what they heard. This reveals if there is any confusion and allows you to refine your messaging immediately.

4. **Structured Agendas**: For meetings, list the points you plan to discuss, the objectives for each topic, and the time allotted. This keeps everyone on the same page and minimizes tangents.

3.6 Encouraging Two-Way Communication

In many organizations, communication flows mostly from the top down. But truly effective workplaces allow information to flow both ways. Encouraging staff to speak up, offer feedback, and ask questions leads to fewer mistakes and stronger solutions.

Practical Ways to Encourage Two-Way Discussion:

- **Open Q&A at the End of Meetings**: Even if you have a packed schedule, setting aside a few minutes for questions shows you value their input.
- **Anonymous Feedback Channels**: Some employees may not feel comfortable voicing concerns publicly. Tools like suggestion boxes or digital surveys can gather honest insights.
- **Team Workshops**: Organize short sessions where everyone can exchange ideas, discuss challenges, and brainstorm improvements.
- **Leadership Rounds**: If you oversee a large department, occasionally visit different teams in their workspace. This casual approach can help people feel at ease when sharing their thoughts.

3.7 Tailoring Communication to Different Audiences

Not everyone in an organization has the same knowledge level or the same interests. An effective leader adapts the message to the listener's background and role. For example, you might explain a company-wide project in less technical detail to a team in finance, focusing on how it affects their budget reporting. Conversely, for the engineering team, you might dig into the technical aspects so they can plan resources accurately.

You should also consider cultural factors, particularly in multinational teams. Humor, gestures, or figures of speech that are acceptable in one place might confuse or offend in another. Taking time to learn about these differences can help avoid misunderstandings and show respect for diverse backgrounds.

3.8 Clarity in Crisis Communication

A crisis can occur at any time: a data breach, a sudden drop in sales, or a public relations issue. Clear communication is vital when uncertainty runs high.

Key Steps in Crisis Communication:

1. **Acknowledge the Problem**: Even if you do not have all the facts, let the team know you are aware of the issue.
2. **State Known Facts**: Stick to verified information to prevent rumors. Avoid speculation.
3. **Outline Initial Actions**: Provide a rough timeline for resolving the issue or gathering more details.
4. **Open Channels**: Encourage questions and feedback to calm fears and show that leadership is taking the matter seriously.

Missteps in crisis communication can trigger widespread panic and mistrust. By handling crises in a transparent and methodical way, you can reduce confusion and keep people working toward solutions.

3.9 Handling Sensitive Information

Leaders often deal with confidential data: financial figures, personal employee information, or strategic plans for new ventures. Striking a balance between openness and confidentiality is a delicate task.

Tips for Managing Sensitive Topics:

- Mark confidential documents clearly and share them only with relevant individuals.
- If you must decline to share certain facts, explain why in a respectful manner. This honesty about your boundaries reinforces credibility.
- Use secure channels for digital communication, such as encrypted email or protected document sharing platforms.

3.10 Nonverbal Communication

Even the most well-chosen words can be overshadowed by tone, facial expressions, and body posture. Research suggests that nonverbal cues can affect how listeners judge the sincerity of your statements. As a boss, be aware of these cues:

1. **Eye Contact**: Looking at someone while you speak shows respect and attentiveness. Avoiding eye contact can make you seem untrustworthy or disinterested.
2. **Tone of Voice**: A calm, steady tone implies confidence, whereas a shaky or rushed tone might show anxiety.
3. **Posture**: Standing or sitting straight while appearing relaxed indicates self-assurance. Slouching can be read as indifference.
4. **Gestures**: Controlled, deliberate gestures reinforce your message. Overly animated or repetitive movements can distract from your words.

3.11 The Role of Preparation

Some leaders try to "wing it" during presentations or staff meetings. This can lead to unclear statements, wasted time, or confusion. Thorough preparation is vital:

1. **Draft Key Points**: Write down the main ideas, not a word-for-word script, so you can speak naturally.
2. **Anticipate Questions**: Think about what people might ask and how you will respond.
3. **Rehearse**: If the stakes are high, practice what you will say. Record yourself or get feedback from someone you trust.
4. **Time Management**: Plan how long each part of your talk or meeting should take. Try not to exceed these limits, to respect others' schedules.

3.12 Building a Communication-Friendly Culture

A single leader's efforts can only do so much. For consistent success, the entire workplace should value clarity and honesty. Encourage team members at all levels to communicate carefully:

- Provide training sessions where employees learn how to craft concise emails or give short presentations.
- Recognize individuals who actively clarify instructions or solve misunderstandings.
- Encourage managers across departments to model strong communication habits, so it becomes a norm rather than a one-time initiative.

3.13 The Long-Term Benefits of Strong Communication

Over time, workplaces that prioritize clarity and purpose in communication enjoy several advantages:

1. **Reduced Errors**: When instructions are straightforward, people make fewer mistakes.
2. **Higher Engagement**: Employees feel more connected to their work when they understand the context behind their tasks.
3. **Stronger Team Spirit**: Open communication helps build trust and reduces tension caused by unclear messages or hidden agendas.
4. **Better Adaptability**: In times of rapid change, a clear communication flow speeds up the organization's response and makes transitions smoother.

3.14 Checking Your Progress

As part of continuous improvement, monitor the state of communication within your team or department:

1. **Surveys and Feedback**: Conduct quick polls to see if workers find instructions easy to understand.
2. **Review Mistakes**: When errors happen, ask if poor communication contributed. If so, correct the process.
3. **Look for Common Complaints**: If you notice repeated questions on the same topic, it suggests your original message was unclear or incomplete.
4. **Regular Self-Evaluation**: Note how you convey important news. If you see people leaving a meeting puzzled, adjust your style.

3.15 Conclusion of Chapter 3

Communication is an essential skill for any great boss. It shapes how your staff perceives goals, organizes tasks, and responds to challenges. By choosing the right channels, aligning messages with clear purposes, and allowing room for feedback, you create a team that can function effectively, even under pressure. Furthermore, when people know you take communication seriously, they are more likely to bring their ideas, concerns, and innovative thinking to the table.

Chapter 4: Setting Goals That Motivate Teams

Goals serve as the compass for every workplace. They give direction, define success, and guide decision-making. However, not all goals are equally effective. Some targets might be too vague, too simple, or too far-fetched, leaving teams unmotivated or confused. This chapter explains how to craft goals that truly inspire results, going beyond the basic tips you might have already encountered. We will explore lesser-known strategies, psychological factors, and hands-on methods to establish targets that lift performance and morale.

4.1 The Importance of Well-Structured Goals

Goals influence behavior and shape priorities. When people know the end result you seek, they can plan tasks more effectively. Goals also help measure progress objectively. For instance, saying "We want to improve sales" is too general. Changing it to "Increase quarterly sales by 15% in the Southeast region" provides a concrete benchmark.

But setting the right goals means more than just picking a number. The goal must connect with the team's reality, resources, and broader organizational plans. If the target is completely unrealistic, employees may lose heart before even starting. If it's too easy, you risk underutilizing talent.

4.2 Mistakes in Goal Setting

Several common pitfalls can undermine the positive impact of goals:

1. **Overly Aggressive Targets**: Leaders sometimes set lofty objectives to push teams to work harder, but goals that far exceed capabilities can lead to burnout, low morale, and even unethical shortcuts.
2. **Neglecting Individual Strengths**: One-size-fits-all goals ignore the varied expertise across a team. This can leave some workers feeling underutilized while overwhelming others.
3. **No Clear Metrics**: Without well-defined metrics, teams can't gauge success. It's hard to know if you're closer to your target or if something needs to change.
4. **Lack of Follow-Up**: Setting targets and then forgetting them is a recipe for failure. Without consistent check-ins, employees may assume the goals are not really important.

4.3 Advanced Goal-Setting Frameworks

Many leaders know about SMART (Specific, Measurable, Achievable, Relevant, Time-Bound). While this is a useful starting point, there are more nuanced approaches:

a) FAST Goals (Frequent, Ambitious, Specific, Transparent)

1. **Frequent**: Instead of setting goals once a year, consider shorter cycles, such as quarterly or monthly. This keeps objectives fresh and allows faster adaptation.
2. **Ambitious**: Set goals slightly beyond comfortable limits but still within reason. This pushes growth without crushing morale.
3. **Specific**: Vague goals lead to guesswork. Clear definitions reduce confusion.
4. **Transparent**: Make progress visible. Let team members see how everyone is doing, which can spark friendly competition or mutual support.

b) OKR (Objectives and Key Results)

Popularized by tech companies, OKRs combine broad objectives with measurable key results. For example:

- **Objective**: Strengthen brand presence in online channels.
- **Key Results**:
    - Improve social media engagement rate by 25%.
    - Launch three new digital advertising campaigns within six months.
    - Increase website traffic by 40% compared to last quarter.

OKRs are short-term, often set every quarter, which promotes agility and frequent evaluation.

4.4 Aligning Team and Individual Goals

Even the best-crafted targets can fail if they don't connect with each person's role. Ideally, each employee sees how their daily tasks link to the main organizational objective. This alignment ensures that everyone's efforts contribute to a unified purpose.

Methods to Achieve Alignment:

1. **Departmental Breakdowns**: Translate company-level goals into department-specific targets. For instance, the marketing team might handle leads, while customer service focuses on retention.
2. **Individual Development Plans**: When reviewing an employee's performance, assign personal targets that feed into bigger company goals. This keeps them engaged and accountable.
3. **Collaborative Planning**: Invite input from employees on how they think they can best support the organization's goals. This fosters commitment because people feel valued.

4.5 Psychological Drivers of Motivation

Goal-setting isn't just a logical process; it also touches on emotional and mental factors that inspire people to push harder. Understanding these drivers helps you craft targets that teams will genuinely want to achieve:

1. **Autonomy**: People often perform better when they have some control over the methods used to reach goals. Instead of micro-managing each step, focus on the end results and let employees decide how to get there.
2. **Mastery**: Many individuals are motivated by improving their skills. If a goal challenges them to learn something new, it becomes more exciting.
3. **Purpose**: If team members see a larger good—whether it's helping society or improving the workplace—they are more likely to stay motivated.
4. **Recognition**: Feeling that achievements are noticed and appreciated can be a powerful driver. This does not mean using the forbidden term that starts with "c" (for praising), but rather acknowledging or rewarding success in meaningful ways.

4.6 Breaking Down Big Goals into Steps

Large, complex targets can overwhelm teams. Breaking them down into milestones or phases allows people to see their progress and feel a sense of accomplishment as they advance. For instance, if the main objective is to open a new branch in another city by year's end, break this into:

- Finalize location and legal documents by the end of Q1.
- Hire key staff by the end of Q2.

- Set up operations and run pilot services by the end of Q3.
- Officially open the branch and start public marketing in Q4.

By laying out these steps, you create realistic checkpoints that keep everyone on track and allow for adjustments if any milestones are delayed.

4.7 Measuring and Tracking Progress

A well-defined goal is only the start. You must also track your team's progress to detect any issues early. Different methods exist:

1. **Project Management Software**: Many platforms offer dashboards that show how tasks move through various stages, making it easier for everyone to see status updates in real time.
2. **Milestone Celebrations**: While you cannot use certain words, you can still mark a completed milestone with a simple team recognition moment or a short mention in a meeting. This acknowledges progress and keeps spirits up.
3. **Regular Check-Ins**: Daily or weekly quick reviews help uncover roadblocks. Managers can then steer resources or adjust timelines accordingly.
4. **Data-Driven Reviews**: Use metrics, charts, or timelines to visually represent progress. This helps people understand the gap between current standing and the final target.

4.8 Adjusting Goals When Needed

Flexibility is not a sign of weakness. Sometimes external factors—economic changes, new competitors, supply chain issues—can shift conditions drastically. A manager who stubbornly sticks to outdated targets risks draining the team's time and morale.

Best Practices for Adjusting Goals:

- Evaluate whether the core objective is still relevant.
- Consult with key stakeholders and team members about the necessary changes.
- Clearly communicate the revised goal and the reason behind the adjustment.

- Update milestones, due dates, or metrics. Ensure everyone understands the new path.

4.9 Avoiding Over-Management

Micro-management can destroy any sense of ownership or motivation. When you set goals, refrain from specifying every small detail. Instead, trust your team to make decisions on how to reach those objectives. If you've hired skilled individuals, give them the freedom to apply their expertise. Overseeing every small move can create anxiety, slow down progress, and limit creativity.

4.10 Connecting Goals with Professional Growth

Another way to boost motivation is to link organizational goals with personal development:

- **Skill Expansion**: If your marketing team's goal is to enter a new market, give a few team members the task of researching local advertising trends. This helps them gain valuable insights and develop new capabilities.
- **Leadership Opportunities**: Offer potential leaders the chance to oversee smaller goal-related projects. This helps you identify who might be ready for a promotion.
- **Peer Learning**: When achieving certain targets, encourage knowledge-sharing sessions so everyone can learn from the experience.

4.11 Involving Stakeholders in Goal Creation

Sometimes, bosses impose targets without consulting the people who will do the actual work. That can lead to unrealistic expectations or lack of buy-in. Involve multiple stakeholders—team leads, frontline workers, subject matter experts—when finalizing goals. This group can provide real-world data on feasibility, resources required, and potential pitfalls.

For instance, if your main objective is to cut production costs by 10%, speak with the operations and procurement staff. They have direct knowledge of where costs can be trimmed and can warn you if certain cuts might harm quality or safety.

4.12 Strategic Goal Sequencing

Not all targets need to happen at once. Proper sequencing avoids spreading resources too thin. Think about which goals must be reached first to pave the way for others. For example, if you want to expand into new international markets, you might first need to bolster your team's language skills or acquire necessary certifications.

Steps to Sequence Goals:

1. Identify any dependencies—tasks or goals that must be finished before another can begin.
2. Determine the priority of each goal based on overall impact and urgency.
3. Create a timeline that cascades from the highest-priority tasks down to the lower ones.
4. Communicate this sequence clearly so all teams understand the order and rationale.

4.13 Handling Team Dynamics in Goal Setting

Groups have unique dynamics that can affect how well they achieve targets. A team with conflicting personalities might fail to meet milestones due to internal disputes. A team with very similar skill sets might lack the creativity to handle sudden challenges. As a boss, recognize these factors and make adjustments:

- Pair employees who have complementary strengths.
- Address interpersonal friction swiftly so it doesn't derail progress.
- If the team lacks certain expertise, consider hiring consultants or arranging temporary training to cover the gap.
- Evaluate workload distribution to ensure no individual is overwhelmed.

4.14 Celebrating Wins

When a team meets a key goal, acknowledge it. This does not require large gestures. A sincere thank you, a mention in a company newsletter, or a quick small event can show people that their work is valued. Although we must avoid certain terms, providing honest recognition goes a long way in boosting morale and reinforcing good habits.

4.15 Dealing with Failure Constructively

Even well-planned goals can go unmet. Instead of punishing the entire team or ignoring the failure, approach it as a learning moment:

1. **Conduct a Post-Mortem**: Review what went wrong, from initial planning to execution. Identify mistakes or external factors.
2. **Own Leadership Gaps**: If leadership decisions contributed to the failure, acknowledge them. This shows integrity and helps rebuild trust.
3. **Refine Future Targets**: Use the findings to set more realistic or better-structured objectives next time.
4. **Encourage Ongoing Learning**: Make sure the team doesn't lose morale. Instead, highlight how the experience will lead to improved strategies.

4.16 Long-Term Vision and Goal Interconnection

Short-term targets should not exist in isolation. They should tie into long-term strategies. A boss who sees the bigger picture can map out how daily or quarterly objectives build toward lasting impact—be it market expansion, technological innovation, or building a brand known for quality.

If your long-term aim is to become an industry leader in customer satisfaction, for instance, each small goal—improving response times, refining product quality, training staff on empathy—should stack up toward that larger vision.

4.17 Using Technology for Better Goal Management

With modern digital tools, tracking performance is more intuitive than ever:

- **Collaboration Tools**: Platforms like Slack, Teams, or Trello can centralize tasks and discussions related to a goal.
- **Analytics Dashboards**: Software that pulls real-time data from various departments allows managers to spot trends and adjust strategies promptly.
- **Automated Reminders**: Notifications can prompt team members about upcoming deadlines or incomplete tasks, reducing the chance of oversight.

- **Visualization Tools**: Graphical representations of progress can motivate people by showing a clear view of how far they've come and what remains.

4.18 Harnessing Constructive Competition

While excessive competition can destroy teamwork, a healthy level of it can spur better performance. If multiple squads are working on parallel goals—like boosting sales in different regions—displaying their results can motivate each group to push a bit harder. However, make sure the focus remains on collective success, not on tearing each other down.

4.19 Keeping the Momentum

Reaching a big goal can sometimes cause a dip in energy afterward. People might relax after the intense push to meet a deadline. Great bosses anticipate this and keep motivation high:

- Introduce the next set of relevant goals promptly.
- Engage in discussions about future plans or expansions.
- Challenge the team to refine or optimize the recent success. For example, if the goal was to launch a new product, propose a follow-up target like hitting a certain number of sales within the first quarter.

4.20 Conclusion of Chapter 4

Setting goals that motivate teams is a critical skill for any boss looking to maximize effectiveness. It involves balancing ambition with realism, tapping into psychological motivators, and structuring objectives in a way that benefits both the organization and the individuals within it. By carefully tracking progress, adjusting when necessary, and acknowledging achievements, you keep your staff focused, engaged, and ready to take on new challenges.

In the upcoming chapters, we will move on to topics such as handling conflict, shaping positive workplace culture, and training team members. Each subject connects back to the foundational elements of good leadership. The ability to set and maintain compelling goals underscores all these areas, acting as a unifying thread that ensures cohesive progress across different facets of management.

Chapter 5: Handling Conflict and Disagreements

A workplace can be a diverse environment, where people of various backgrounds and viewpoints come together. This diversity often leads to richer ideas and stronger results, but it can also lead to clashes and misunderstandings. As a boss, your job involves making sure conflicts do not spin out of control. Effective conflict management is not just about staying calm; it requires insight into hidden triggers, group dynamics, and smart strategies that promote fairness. This chapter examines methods for reducing friction, while also digging into advanced tactics that many leaders overlook. By the end, you will have a deeper understanding of why conflicts happen and how to solve them without harming team unity.

5.1 Understanding the Roots of Conflict

Many people blame personality differences as the primary cause of clashes. However, deeper factors can spark tension. Some of these include:

1. **Resource Struggles**: Team members might argue if they feel they are competing for limited tools, funding, or recognition.
2. **Role Overlap**: When two people have unclear or overlapping duties, each one may feel the other is stepping on their territory.
3. **Communication Gaps**: Vague instructions or half-shared information can breed misunderstandings that later turn into bigger disputes.
4. **Value Clashes**: Sometimes differences in core beliefs—like how to treat clients, how to prioritize tasks, or how to manage time—cause friction.

A boss who can spot these roots early is more likely to address them before they grow into major problems.

5.2 The Cost of Unresolved Conflict

Unresolved disputes do more than spoil the mood in the office. They can reduce productivity, lead to staff quitting, and harm the reputation of your department or company. When people are preoccupied with their disagreements, they have less energy for solving real work issues. Tensions can also reach clients or project partners, causing them to question the reliability of your team. As a result, valuable projects might slip away, and overall morale could drop.

Understanding these consequences is a key step in taking conflict resolution seriously. A wise boss sees that ignoring problems can be far more expensive than handling them quickly and directly.

5.3 Early Detection Methods

Many disagreements give warning signs before they grow. Observing for these signals can help a boss act before anger escalates:

- **Avoidance Behaviors**: If a team member constantly avoids another, refuses to speak during group meetings, or hides data that should be shared, it might be a sign of brewing tension.
- **Body Language**: Rolling eyes, tense posture, or forced smiles during group interactions can indicate deeper issues.
- **Repeated Complaints**: When the same employee raises the same type of complaint about a teammate or process, it suggests an underlying conflict that needs attention.
- **Sudden Drops in Performance**: A previously enthusiastic worker may start showing apathy or frustration, possibly due to interpersonal friction.

Spotting these signals provides you with the chance to intervene while problems are still small and easier to solve.

5.4 Addressing Conflict: A Structured Approach

Instead of relying on emotional appeals, a structured approach helps ensure fairness and consistency:

1. **Gather Facts**: Start by speaking separately with those involved. Ask open-ended questions about what happened, how it started, and how it affects work. Avoid blaming or taking sides.

2. **Identify the Core Issue**: Figure out whether the conflict arises from unclear tasks, clashing goals, or personal resentment.
3. **Guide a Face-to-Face Discussion**: Bring the parties together and set ground rules, such as no interruptions and respectful speech. Allow each person to share their point of view.
4. **Seek Agreement on the Problem Statement**: Both sides must agree on what the main issue is. This step alone can reduce tension because it requires them to work together in defining the problem.
5. **Generate Solutions**: Encourage participants to brainstorm solutions. The boss acts as a guide, helping them examine the pros and cons of each option.
6. **Decide and Implement**: Once a solution is chosen, outline the steps each person will take. Document it to avoid confusion later.
7. **Follow Up**: Check in after some time to see if the tension has reduced and if the solution remains effective.

Using a system like this not only resolves the immediate conflict but also teaches employees how to address future disagreements in a constructive manner.

5.5 Communicating Without Triggering Defensiveness

When people feel attacked, they often shut down or strike back. Effective bosses learn ways to bring up hard issues without provoking defensiveness:

- **Use "I" Statements**: Say "I've noticed deadlines have been missed and want to understand what's happening," rather than "You are always late with your work."
- **Practice Active Listening**: While the other person speaks, show genuine focus. Nod your head, keep eye contact, and summarize what they say to confirm you understand.
- **Avoid Absolute Words**: Words like "always" or "never" can exaggerate the situation and cause more conflict.
- **Stay Neutral in Tone**: Keep your voice steady and calm. Do not allow frustration to color your words.

These methods reassure employees that your aim is to address the problem, not to place blame or shame anyone.

5.6 The Role of Empathy and Boundaries

Empathy allows you to see a conflict through the eyes of those involved. However, empathy does not mean letting people get away with poor behavior. The best bosses balance understanding with clear boundaries:

- **Show Genuine Concern**: If someone expresses stress over workload, take it seriously. Ask questions to understand their point of view.
- **Set Limits**: Make it clear that certain actions—like personal insults or withholding critical info—are not permitted in the workplace.
- **Offer Support**: If the conflict is tied to personal issues (e.g., family problems affecting a staff member's attitude), direct them to any available employee assistance resources.
- **Link Empathy to Solutions**: After hearing someone's concerns, explain how those insights help shape a plan to fix the conflict. This shows empathy in action, not just in words.

5.7 Handling Conflict Between You and an Employee

Bosses are not immune to friction with staff. Whether it's a difference in opinions about strategy or a misunderstanding about performance feedback, conflicts can arise:

1. **Be Willing to Self-Assess**: Reflect on whether your management style or communication contributed to the tension.
2. **Invite a Trusted Mediator**: If the situation is severe, ask a neutral party (e.g., an HR representative) to facilitate the discussion.
3. **Focus on Shared Goals**: Remind the employee that both of you want the team and the company to succeed. Find common ground to start rebuilding trust.
4. **Document Agreements**: Put any resolutions in writing, so both sides have clear reference points. This reduces the chance of future disagreements over what was discussed.

When employees see their boss also follows a fair process, it encourages them to handle their own disputes more responsibly.

5.8 Inter-Departmental Tensions

Sometimes, conflict happens not just between individuals but also between entire teams or departments. Sales might blame production for not meeting deadlines, while production says sales promised unrealistic timelines. In these cases:

- **Bring Key Leaders Together**: Have the heads of each department discuss the points of friction.
- **Map Out the Process**: Visualize the workflow from one department to the next. Identify bottlenecks and see where responsibilities might overlap or clash.
- **Agree on Shared Metrics**: If both sales and production are graded on overall success (e.g., combined on-time delivery rate), they have a reason to collaborate rather than fight.
- **Plan Shared Projects**: Assign tasks that require both sides to work toward one outcome. This helps them understand each other's challenges and find ways to cooperate.

By focusing on shared objectives, departments can work in harmony instead of shifting blame.

5.9 Cross-Cultural Differences

In a global or multinational company, cultural differences can sometimes spark friction. Communication norms, hierarchy views, or approaches to problem-solving may vary significantly. To minimize conflicts:

- **Offer Cultural Awareness Sessions**: Teach staff about different customs and communication styles found within the organization.
- **Create Mixed Teams**: Encourage collaboration across cultural lines so employees can learn from each other's work habits.
- **Show Patience with Language Barriers**: If team members are not fully fluent in the common company language, allow extra time for clarifications. Misunderstandings often arise from simple language issues.

- **Model Inclusivity**: As a boss, show respect for cultural variety. Pronounce names correctly, ask about cultural celebrations, and make everyone feel valued.

5.10 When to Seek Outside Help

Not all conflicts can be fixed internally. If personal grudges or deep-rooted issues exist, professional mediators might be needed. An external mediator or facilitator can listen objectively and lead structured discussions that might be hard for internal leaders to guide fairly. Such a step might appear extreme, but it can save time, reduce emotional stress, and prevent the loss of strong employees.

5.11 Balancing Informal and Formal Conflict Resolution

Deciding whether to address a problem casually or through formal channels can be tricky. Some leaders prefer informal chats first, to see if a simple conversation can fix things. If the conflict involves alleged harassment or serious misconduct, a more official approach is necessary.

- **Informal Measures**: Quick private talks, reshuffling minor tasks, or encouraging a heartfelt apology can often resolve smaller or new issues.
- **Formal Measures**: When trust is broken, behavior crosses ethical lines, or repeated attempts have failed, it might be time to escalate. Formal measures can include HR-led investigations, written warnings, or even performance improvement plans.

5.12 Teaching Employees Conflict-Resolution Skills

Rather than stepping in each time a disagreement comes up, teach staff how to address issues on their own:

1. **Group Workshops**: Hold training sessions on conflict resolution techniques, such as listening exercises and structured problem-solving.

2. **Role-Playing**: Have employees act out tough scenarios in a safe environment. This allows them to practice de-escalation and negotiation.
3. **Internal Mentors**: Encourage experienced members to coach newer colleagues on handling everyday disputes in a calm, fair manner.
4. **Consistent Reinforcement**: Whenever a conflict arises and is resolved well, highlight what worked about that approach. This shows the entire team positive examples.

Over time, you build a workforce that can solve small conflicts independently, saving you energy for higher-level leadership tasks.

5.13 Handling Ongoing Tensions

Some conflicts simmer for a long time, with small daily triggers keeping them alive. These might include personality mismatches or long-standing mistrust:

- **Periodic Check-Ins**: If you suspect continued resentment, schedule quick, private chats to see if any new issues have surfaced.
- **Shift Team Assignments**: Sometimes, separating people who constantly clash is best for productivity, provided the tasks still match their skills.
- **Revisit Past Agreements**: Remind team members of the commitments they made during mediation sessions. Ask if they still stand by those commitments.
- **Rebuild Relationships**: Suggest ways they can cooperate on low-risk tasks to gradually rebuild confidence in each other's reliability.

5.14 Handling Conflict in Virtual Teams

As remote work becomes more common, conflicts can arise without the face-to-face conversations that often catch misunderstandings early. Remote employees might misread written messages, or time zone gaps might delay clarifications. To address this:

1. **Set Clear Communication Norms**: Decide on response times, preferred channels for urgent vs. non-urgent matters, and standard meeting schedules.

2. **Use Video Calls**: Relying solely on text can escalate misunderstandings. Seeing facial expressions can help both sides interpret each other better.
3. **Be Aware of Tone**: Written words might sound harsher than intended. Encourage staff to use polite language and add clarifying notes if the topic is complex.
4. **Encourage Informal Chats**: Remote teams lose the casual "water-cooler" talk" that helps people build bonds. Set up optional small group calls or chat rooms where employees can relax and get to know each other better.

5.15 Setting a Zero-Tolerance Standard for Harmful Behavior

While most conflicts can be managed through discussion, certain behaviors must never be allowed. These include bullying, harassment, and discriminatory conduct. As a boss:

- **Make Policies Clear**: Clearly state that harassment or discrimination will lead to serious consequences.
- **Respond Swiftly**: If a complaint arises, investigate quickly and thoroughly. Delaying sends the wrong message.
- **Protect Confidentiality**: If individuals fear retaliation for reporting, they may stay silent, allowing harmful behavior to continue.
- **Be Ready to Remove Toxic Influences**: In cases where someone repeatedly violates core standards, termination may be necessary to safeguard the team.

5.16 Psychological Aspects of Conflict

Beyond practical steps, conflict often has an emotional component. Cognitive biases, personal triggers, or past experiences can intensify reactions. Being aware of these mental factors gives you extra tools for resolution:

- **Confirmation Bias**: People may only notice data that supports their side, ignoring opposing evidence. Encourage everyone to list facts for and against each viewpoint.

- **Attribution Error**: Workers might blame personal traits for someone else's mistake, while excusing their own missteps as situational. Ask each person to consider external factors that might have contributed to the issue.
- **Emotional Contagion**: Strong emotions can spread through a group, raising tension. Maintain a calm presence and encourage open discussions to neutralize negative energy.

Recognizing these psychological triggers helps you guide discussions more effectively.

5.17 Keeping Records

A boss who relies on memory alone risks confusion or disputes about what was said. Keep a clear record of major conflict-resolution steps:

1. **Email Summaries**: After a mediation or meeting, send a concise email listing the key points and any agreed-upon actions.
2. **Shared Documents**: If the conflict involves processes or deadlines, store updated guidelines in a shared folder everyone can access.
3. **Performance Records**: If an ongoing conflict affects performance, document your observations for future reference or HR involvement.
4. **Protect Privacy**: Keep these records confidential, sharing only with relevant parties.

Documenting ensures clarity and helps avoid "he said, she said" scenarios later.

5.18 Rebuilding Trust After Conflict

A single conflict can damage trust for weeks or months. Your efforts should not stop once a handshake is made or an agreement is signed:

- **Offer Constructive Feedback**: Praise people for using good communication methods, and point out any ongoing issues that might still spark friction.

- **Assign Collaborative Tasks**: Encourage the parties to work together on projects that let them see each other's strengths.
- **Recognize Improvements**: When you see progress—like calmer communication or willingness to share resources—offer genuine recognition.
- **Encourage Social Interaction**: Without using forbidden terms, you can still support low-key team-building activities or casual get-togethers. These can help people move past old grudges.

Gradual steps and consistent follow-up can often mend damaged relationships.

5.19 Training Leaders to Handle Conflict

If your organization has several managers, each one should learn effective conflict-resolution skills. Host sessions where managers can:

- Practice real scenarios they might face.
- Learn the same structured approach to conflicts for consistency.
- Share their own experiences in a supportive setting.
- Get advice from experts or senior leaders who have tackled complex problems.

When all leaders use the same guidelines, you develop a unified approach that employees recognize and trust.

5.20 Conclusion of Chapter 5

Conflicts are inevitable in any workplace, but they do not have to be destructive. With the right mindset, clear strategies, and fair processes, a boss can turn disputes into chances for growth and improved understanding. Early detection, structured mediation, empathy balanced with firm standards, and proper follow-up all play a role in ensuring disagreements do not derail productivity. By acknowledging the emotional side of conflict, documenting each step, and training others in your methods, you create an environment where disagreements are handled quickly and fairly.

Chapter 6: Fostering a Healthy Workplace Culture

A healthy workplace culture is not about fancy perks, slogans on the wall, or forced social gatherings. It is about building an environment where employees feel respected, engaged, and able to do their best. As a boss, you have a major influence on the mood and standards in your department or organization. This chapter explains the hidden levers that shape workplace culture. We will explore the reasons some attempts to improve culture fail, then offer advanced methods for creating genuine improvement that stands the test of time.

6.1 Defining Workplace Culture in Practical Terms

Culture is often defined by abstract ideas like "the way we do things here." But in a practical sense, it shows up as:

1. **Daily Behaviors**: How employees talk to each other, the tone of meetings, and how conflicts are handled.
2. **Core Beliefs**: The shared sense of what is important, such as quality, safety, or customer happiness.
3. **Symbols and Rituals**: Company events or traditions that reinforce certain messages.
4. **Decision-Making Style**: Whether decisions are made collaboratively or handed down from the top with no discussion.

You will know the culture is healthy when employees trust leadership, find meaning in their work, and generally communicate openly—even about difficult topics.

6.2 Why Culture Matters

Culture affects nearly every aspect of the organization:

- **Talent Retention**: Good employees are more likely to stay when they feel a strong sense of belonging.

- **Performance and Creativity**: A supportive culture leads to higher productivity and more willingness to share fresh ideas.
- **Public Image**: Clients, partners, and job seekers often judge a company by how it treats its workforce.
- **Resilience in Hard Times**: When the going gets tough—such as in market downturns or unexpected crises—a healthy culture helps teams band together and keep morale steady.

Building a strong culture is thus a strategic investment, not just a "nice to have."

6.3 Recognizing Cultural Red Flags

Sometimes culture starts to deteriorate without obvious signs at first. But staying alert to these red flags can help you catch issues early:

- **High Turnover**: If skilled employees keep leaving, it might be more than just pay. They might be escaping toxic relationships or unclear direction.
- **Absenteeism**: Regular sick days or late arrivals may indicate low morale, burnout, or lack of engagement.
- **Silence in Meetings**: If nobody raises concerns or offers new ideas, fear or apathy could be stifling innovation.
- **Gossip and Rumors**: When people do not feel safe sharing concerns openly, they may turn to hushed conversations that erode trust.
- **Resistance to Change**: While some caution is normal, outright refusal to adapt could signal a culture that punishes risk-taking or dismisses new ideas.

6.4 Laying the Foundation: Values and Principles

Many organizations list "integrity," "teamwork," or "customer focus" as their core values. But a common mistake is to leave these values on paper rather than weaving them into daily life:

- **Connect Values to Behaviors**: If you say "we value integrity," clarify how it applies to tasks. For instance, refusing to overlook a product flaw, even if it means missing a deadline.

- **Reward Actual Practice**: Recognize employees who show these values in action. For instance, a staff member who corrects a billing mistake in the company's favor should be praised for honesty.
- **Hire and Promote for Values**: During recruitment or promotions, evaluate candidates not just for skills but also how well they fit with the culture you want.

By making values practical, you prevent them from becoming empty buzzwords.

6.5 The Leader's Role in Modeling Culture

Employees watch their bosses carefully. If you say "We value respect," but then shout at people in meetings, your words lose credibility. Modeling is crucial:

1. **Self-Awareness**: Recognize that your daily decisions and actions signal to employees what is truly important.
2. **Accountability**: Apologize when you fail to live up to the standards you set. This shows authenticity.
3. **Fair Decision-Making**: Apply rules and policies equally, no matter who is involved. Favoritism will quickly wreck trust.
4. **Visibility**: Spend time with the team, whether through casual conversations, regular check-ins, or visits to different departments. This presence shows you care about the group's experiences.

6.6 Communication Styles That Nurture Positive Culture

Workplaces that thrive tend to have open and respectful dialogue. To foster this:

- **Transparency with Context**: Give the "why" behind decisions. People often respond better when they see the full picture.
- **Approachable Tone**: Speak in plain language, invite questions, and listen. Avoid jargon that could confuse or alienate staff.
- **Regular Feedback Cycles**: Create a culture where employees receive constructive feedback frequently, not just once a year. Offer tools for self-improvement.

- **Praise Done Right**: When praising, be specific. Point out the behavior and why it matters, rather than using generic compliments.

6.7 Building Psychological Safety

Psychological safety means employees feel safe taking risks, voicing opinions, and admitting errors without fear of punishment. This is crucial for innovation and continuous improvement. As a boss, you can:

- **Encourage Candor**: Ask for critical viewpoints and thank people for raising tough questions.
- **Normalize Honest Mistakes**: When an error occurs, focus on the lesson learned and share it so others can avoid repeating the same mistake.
- **Respect Confidentiality**: If employees share personal or sensitive info, keep it private. Breaking that trust can cause long-term harm.
- **Set Group Norms**: Make it clear in meetings that interruptions or mocking remarks are not allowed.

When people feel safe, they bring their best ideas and effort to the table.

6.8 Encouraging Cross-Functional Collaboration

A healthy culture often breaks down silos between departments, letting people collaborate with ease:

1. **Shared Projects**: Assign tasks that require employees from different specialties to work together.
2. **Open Workspaces**: Physical or digital setups that allow for informal chats across teams can spark unexpected partnerships.
3. **Rotational Programs**: Let employees spend short periods in other departments to gain a better understanding of broader operations.
4. **Joint Goals**: If multiple teams share responsibility for certain performance metrics, they have a reason to help one another rather than compete.

6.9 Support Systems for Employee Well-Being

A major aspect of culture is how well an organization supports its people's overall health:

- **Flexible Work Options**: If possible, offer remote or hybrid arrangements, especially for employees who have personal obligations or long commutes.
- **Resources for Stress Management**: Provide access to counseling or mental health programs.
- **Reasonable Workloads**: Set realistic deadlines and encourage breaks to prevent burnout.
- **Recognition of Life Events**: A quick genuine note to acknowledge a key event (e.g., welcoming a child, caring for a relative) shows understanding.

These measures let employees know they are seen as human beings, not just worker units.

6.10 Handling Subcultures

Large organizations can develop pockets or "subcultures," each with its own norms. A research department might have a more relaxed atmosphere, while the sales team thrives on high energy. This is normal, but problems arise if a subculture runs against the overall principles. Keep subcultures aligned by:

1. **Checking the Overall Core Values**: Ensure each subculture doesn't contradict essential guidelines like respect or openness.
2. **Rotating Leadership**: If possible, move managers across different teams to share practices and unify standards.
3. **Periodic Team-Building Across Departments**: Let subcultures mix so they understand each other's ways of working.

6.11 Avoiding Superficial Fixes

Some companies think that adding games in the break room or holding a corporate party will "fix" the culture. Such perks might be short-lived if deeper issues remain. Instead:

- **Address Real Pain Points**: If employees feel undervalued or micromanaged, tackle those concerns first.
- **Gather Honest Feedback**: Anonymous surveys or confidential listening sessions can reveal what truly bothers people.
- **Prioritize Action Over Hype**: Show measurable changes. For example, if the biggest complaint is heavy workloads, reorganize tasks or hire more help rather than simply offering free snacks.

Surface-level efforts may bring momentary smiles, but real cultural strength comes from lasting improvements.

6.12 Encouraging Meaningful Mentorship

A culture that promotes learning and growth is more likely to retain skilled talent. Mentorship programs can help:

- **Pair Veteran Employees with New Hires**: This transfer of knowledge eases onboarding and builds bonds.
- **Cross-Level Mentorship**: A strong performer at a lower level might teach a manager about new technical tools, while the manager can share leadership lessons.
- **Set Clear Goals**: Mentors and mentees should define what they hope to achieve from the relationship.
- **Recognize Mentors**: Show appreciation for those who take the time to guide others. This encourages more employees to volunteer as mentors.

6.13 Handling Resistance to Culture Changes

Any shift in culture can meet pushback. Employees who benefited from the old ways might fear losing status or comfort. Strategies to manage this include:

1. **Clearly Explain the Reason for Change**: Show how the new culture aligns with company success and employee well-being.
2. **Involve Skeptics**: Invite vocal critics to help refine new policies. This can bring them on board or reveal legitimate concerns.

3. **Offer Training**: If culture changes demand new skills—like conflict resolution or collaborative project management—provide resources so people can adapt.
4. **Be Patient but Firm**: While it takes time for habits to shift, repeated sabotage of the new culture should have consequences.

6.14 Measuring Cultural Health

Culture might feel intangible, but certain indicators can help track improvement:

- **Engagement Surveys**: Ask employees about job satisfaction, sense of purpose, and trust in leadership.
- **Turnover and Absentee Rates**: Decreases in these rates often signal a healthier environment.
- **Referrals and Employee Recommendations**: If your staff suggests the company to friends or professional contacts, they likely have confidence in the culture.
- **Performance Metrics**: Watch for increases in productivity, quality, or customer satisfaction as cultural changes take root.

6.15 Technology's Role in Culture

While technology alone cannot solve cultural problems, it can aid or hinder your efforts:

- **Communication Tools**: Apps like Slack or Teams can improve sharing of updates but can also overwhelm people with messages if not managed well.
- **Project Management Platforms**: These make work more transparent and reduce confusion about tasks and deadlines.
- **Digital Recognition**: Simple systems that allow colleagues to thank each other can reinforce positive interactions.
- **Remote Culture**: For distributed teams, video conferencing and shared online spaces keep everyone connected, but be sure to schedule enough synchronous time to build trust.

6.16 The Boss as a Cultural Architect

Being a boss means you shape the culture, whether you realize it or not. Every policy you set, every decision you make, and every reaction you show to problems sends a message:

1. **Champion the Right Behaviors**: When you see an employee handling a tough situation with composure, highlight it as an example for others.
2. **Stay Informed**: Regularly talk to people at different levels to see how they feel about the culture. Don't rely solely on top-down reports.
3. **Keep Updating Your Own Skills**: Whether it's learning about new leadership approaches or taking a course on emotional intelligence, continual growth prevents you from becoming an obstacle to progress.
4. **Challenge Unproductive Traditions**: If your department has always done something that conflicts with modern standards of respect or collaboration, question why it continues.

6.17 Dealing with Failure Constructively

A workplace that punishes mistakes harshly will struggle to grow. Instead, shift the mindset around failure:

- **Focus on Insights**: Ask what the team learned when a project misses its targets. Document these insights for future reference.
- **Share Your Own Slip-Ups**: When appropriate, mention times you made a mistake and how you addressed it. This sets an example of honest reflection.
- **Set Learning Goals**: Encourage employees to set skill-based objectives, not just output targets. That way, even if a project fails, they have gained new abilities.
- **Recognize Efforts in Challenging Tasks**: Even if results were less than expected, note that taking on a risky project was itself a demonstration of initiative.

6.18 Onboarding New Hires into the Culture

New employees quickly learn the real culture—sometimes through observations and unofficial chatter. Make sure you provide a clearer path:

1. **Structured Welcome**: Assign a buddy who introduces them to key people and answers casual questions.
2. **Explain Cultural Norms**: During orientation, go beyond job duties. Cover how people usually give feedback, how to handle disagreements, and where to find resources.
3. **Rapid Inclusion**: Invite them to small group discussions or relevant team meetings so they feel integrated, not isolated.
4. **Check-In**: After a month or two, follow up to see if they have encountered any cultural confusion. This helps correct misunderstandings early.

6.19 Long-Term Sustainability

Cultural improvements are not a one-time project. They need consistent focus:

- **Revisit Values Periodically**: Update any guidelines to match the realities of the changing work environment.
- **Succession Planning**: Prepare future leaders who share the same commitment to a healthy culture.
- **Listen to External Voices**: Client feedback or industry best practices can help you refine your culture to stay competitive and ethical.
- **Stay Alert**: As the team grows or merges with others, potential conflicts might emerge. Regular evaluations help you adjust quickly.

6.20 Conclusion of Chapter 6

A healthy workplace culture forms the backbone of any successful organization. By being intentional about values, rewarding positive behaviors, and supporting employees in their professional and personal well-being, you lay the groundwork for long-term stability. While perks and fun events can add a spark, real cultural strength comes from daily actions, fair leadership, and open communication. When people feel safe, respected, and motivated, they are more likely to innovate and work together toward shared goals.

Chapter 7: Training and Developing Team Members

Any business relies on the skills and motivation of the people who do the work every day. A boss who wants long-term success must ensure that team members do not stagnate and fall behind as the industry moves forward. Training programs and professional development efforts are key ingredients in keeping talent strong, preventing skill gaps, and building a loyal workforce. This chapter will discuss strategies for assessing skill needs, creating robust development plans, and moving beyond basic, one-size-fits-all training sessions. By the end, you will have a strong framework for growing the knowledge and expertise of your team, without repeating general tips that everyone already knows.

7.1 Why Training and Development Matter More Than Ever

In times of fast-paced change, the methods and tools that worked five years ago may already be outdated. Customers demand new solutions, technology evolves monthly, and competitors adopt advanced processes. If employees do not receive regular training, they will be less equipped to tackle modern tasks. Moreover:

1. **Retention of Top Talent**: Skilled employees expect to learn and advance in their careers. A lack of growth opportunities can prompt them to look elsewhere.
2. **Adaptability**: Well-trained teams can pivot quickly when business strategies shift or when new products enter the market.
3. **Quality and Efficiency**: Continuing education improves the quality of outputs and reduces errors.
4. **Future Leadership**: Today's well-trained staff can become tomorrow's managers or specialists who can lead important initiatives.

Recognizing these benefits is the first step in building a strong training culture.

7.2 Recognizing Skill Gaps

Not all employees require the same training. Some may be excellent at technology but lack communication skills. Others may excel at creative thinking yet struggle with project management. Effective bosses spend time identifying the precise skill gaps within their team.

Methods for Identifying Skill Gaps:

- **Performance Reviews**: Go beyond rating forms and hold genuine conversations about where employees feel they need improvement.
- **Observation**: Watch employees in daily tasks. Do they struggle with certain tools or processes?
- **Customer Feedback**: If customers point out repetitive mistakes, it might indicate a lack of training in a key area.
- **Team Discussions**: Ask employees which skills they believe are missing. They might see a need that you have not noticed.
- **Benchmarking**: Compare your team's skill levels to industry standards or to top competitors. If your peers in other companies are adopting a certain technique, assess whether your employees have that same ability.

Once you map these gaps, you can structure a targeted training plan that addresses real needs, rather than generic topics.

7.3 Creating a Tailored Training Plan

Many companies make the error of conducting broad training sessions that do not relate to individual roles. A better approach is to customize training based on both the organization's overall strategy and the specific needs of each person.

1. **Link to Business Goals**: If your main objective is to expand into digital marketing, focus on analytics tools, social media strategies, and content planning.
2. **Segment the Audience**: Group employees by their roles or skill levels. For instance, a separate track for new hires learning basic processes, versus a specialized track for senior employees learning advanced management or high-level software.

3. **Blend Different Methods**: Combine classroom-style workshops, online modules, reading materials, and hands-on exercises. People learn in varied ways, so a mix of teaching approaches helps.
4. **Check Resources**: Evaluate your budget, the availability of internal experts, and the time employees can devote without harming productivity.

By building a plan that aligns with business targets and individual growth, you increase the chance of real impact.

7.4 The 70-20-10 Model and Other Frameworks

Some organizations follow the 70-20-10 principle:

- **70%** of learning occurs through on-the-job experiences, such as tackling new projects and responsibilities.
- **20%** happens through coaching or mentoring, where employees receive guidance from supervisors or more experienced colleagues.
- **10%** comes from formal courses or structured training.

Although this is not universal, it highlights the idea that most development happens through doing. Formal training is important, but real progress emerges when employees apply knowledge in their daily tasks. Other frameworks might put different weight on each category, but the central message remains: combine theory with practical experience and support from mentors.

7.5 Practical On-the-Job Training Methods

On-the-job learning can be one of the most powerful ways to build skills quickly and with minimal disruption:

1. **Shadowing**: A less experienced employee observes a specialist or top performer during actual tasks. After a while, they switch roles, with the specialist supervising while the learner executes tasks.
2. **Project Assignments**: Assign employees to projects that stretch their current skills. This approach forces them to pick up new techniques and fosters accountability.

3. **Rotations**: Rotate staff across departments so they gain exposure to different workflows. This is especially valuable for future managers who need a broad view of the company.
4. **Peer Reviews**: Encourage employees to review each other's work. Constructive peer feedback sharpens skills and also fosters collaboration.
5. **Cross-Training**: Let employees learn tasks usually done by their co-workers. This prevents workflow disruptions if someone is absent and gives staff members a better sense of the entire process.

When managed well, these methods can accelerate learning without requiring a large training budget.

7.6 Formal Learning Opportunities

Although on-the-job methods are powerful, formal programs still have a place:

1. **Workshops and Seminars**: In-person workshops allow hands-on practice, plus the chance to ask questions directly.
2. **Online Courses**: Many platforms offer flexible lessons that employees can handle at their own pace. Make sure the courses are high quality and aligned with company needs.
3. **Industry Conferences**: This can be a chance for employees to learn best practices, explore new trends, and make valuable connections.
4. **Certifications**: For technical fields like IT or accounting, recognized certifications help maintain standards and give employees a sense of achievement.
5. **In-House Training Sessions**: If you have experts on staff, invite them to teach. This can be more targeted than external classes, and also helps the internal expert develop their own teaching and leadership skills.

Selecting the right mix of formal and informal programs ensures that employees gain both foundational knowledge and the ability to apply it in real situations.

7.7 The Role of Coaching and Mentoring

Coaching and mentoring can be transformative in a person's career, and bosses who encourage these relationships often see productivity and morale rise. However, it is important to distinguish between them:

- **Coaching** is often short-term and focused on specific performance targets. A coach helps an employee improve in a particular area, like presentation skills or time management, using structured sessions with clear goals and follow-up.
- **Mentoring** is more long-term and broader. A mentor shares not just job-related insights but also wider career advice, serving as a role model and confidant.

Tips for Setting Up a Successful Mentoring Program:

1. **Match Mentors and Mentees Carefully**: Pair people who share interests or where the mentor's expertise matches the mentee's growth goals.
2. **Clarify Expectations**: Outline how often they will meet, what topics are open for discussion, and how progress will be measured.
3. **Provide Mentor Training**: Not everyone automatically knows how to be a good mentor. Simple guidelines on asking questions, providing feedback, and respecting boundaries can help them succeed.
4. **Recognize Mentor Contributions**: Mentoring takes time and effort. Show genuine appreciation for those who invest in developing others.

7.8 Tracking and Measuring Training Impact

One of the biggest mistakes bosses make is launching training initiatives without a plan to assess results. You can measure training effectiveness in several ways:

1. **Pre- and Post-Assessments**: Test or survey employees before and after the training to gauge improvements in knowledge or skills.
2. **Performance Metrics**: If the training was about reducing errors in manufacturing, for example, track error rates over time. If the numbers drop, the training likely had a positive effect.
3. **Feedback from Participants**: Ask employees how they are applying their new skills and what might still be confusing.

4. **Supervisor Observations**: Have supervisors watch for behavioral changes in areas like teamwork, problem-solving, or innovation.
5. **ROI Analysis**: In more formal settings, some companies try to quantify the return on investment by calculating costs and benefits (such as fewer mistakes or higher productivity).

Collecting data not only justifies the training budget but also helps refine future programs.

7.9 Avoiding Common Pitfalls

Training can fail if handled incorrectly. Look out for these mistakes:

1. **Overloading Employees**: Scheduling training during peak workload seasons can cause stress and discourage learning.
2. **Mandatory One-Size-Fits-All Sessions**: Requiring everyone to attend the same training, regardless of relevance, wastes time and money.
3. **Ignoring Post-Training Reinforcement**: Skills gained in a workshop may fade if employees never practice them afterward.
4. **Not Aligning with Real Needs**: Teaching advanced analytics to a team that rarely handles data might yield little benefit.
5. **Focusing Only on Weaknesses**: While addressing gaps is good, don't forget to build on strengths. Sometimes honing existing talent can be more effective than trying to fix every shortcoming.

By staying aware of these errors, you can design programs that truly elevate the team.

7.10 Creating a Culture of Continuous Learning

Rather than viewing training as an occasional activity, top-performing companies treat it as an ongoing priority. Here are some methods for nurturing that approach:

- **Regular Knowledge-Sharing Sessions**: Have employees take turns presenting short talks on what they have learned or discovered.

- **Internal Newsletters or Forums**: Encourage staff to share tips, articles, or insights they picked up from outside reading or conferences.
- **Small Learning Groups**: A few employees can form a reading circle around a topic, meet weekly, and apply what they learn.
- **Technology Platforms**: Use a learning management system that centralizes courses, tracks progress, and suggests next steps.
- **Management Support**: Ensure managers at every level set aside time and budget for skill growth. If employees see that their bosses do not prioritize learning, they will not prioritize it either.

When continuous improvement becomes a standard part of the work week, employees stay curious and adaptable.

7.11 Advanced Methods for Employee Development

For ambitious bosses looking to go beyond simple training, consider these approaches:

1. **Action Learning Projects**: Form small groups to solve a real, pressing problem the company faces. While addressing the problem, participants learn teamwork, research, and leadership skills.
2. **Innovation Labs**: Dedicate a portion of the schedule for employees to experiment with new ideas or technologies. Provide basic guidance, but let them explore.
3. **Reverse Mentoring**: Younger or junior employees might teach senior staff about emerging tech trends, social media, or modern user habits. This flips the usual mentor-mentee relationship and keeps senior employees from falling behind.
4. **Learning Rewards**: While you cannot use a certain word beginning with "c" that would mean to rejoice, you can still highlight learning achievements in newsletters or departmental meetings. Show that the organization values new knowledge, not just output.

Such methods require thoughtful setup, but they can push your team's capabilities to new levels.

7.12 Balancing Costs and Benefits

Training can be expensive in terms of both money and time. A boss must weigh these costs against potential benefits:

- **Choose the Right Format**: If an in-person seminar is too pricey, consider online classes or in-house experts.
- **Select High-Value Topics**: Pick subjects likely to bring tangible advantages. Basic computer literacy might be essential for administrative staff, while advanced negotiation skills might be key for sales teams.
- **Set Clear Expectations**: If a company covers the cost of certifications or degrees, be clear about any required payback if the employee leaves soon after.
- **Look for Collaboration**: Sometimes, teaming up with partner companies or industry associations reduces training expenses through shared workshops.

By focusing on the best possible return, you ensure training investments make sense for the business.

7.13 Involving Employees in Their Own Development

Employees should not be mere recipients of training plans imposed from above. Involving them in the process leads to stronger results:

- **Self-Assessment**: Encourage employees to evaluate their strengths and gaps. They may uncover areas that you had overlooked.
- **Personal Goals**: During performance reviews, ask employees about their career aspirations. This helps match training options to their long-term interests.
- **Learning Contracts**: Have employees propose their learning objectives, methods, and timelines. Review and approve these plans, offering resources and guidance along the way.
- **Ongoing Check-Ins**: Periodically discuss whether they are meeting their learning commitments. Celebrate small milestones and adjust plans if needed.

When people have a say in what they learn, they are more motivated to make full use of those opportunities.

7.14 Partnering with External Experts

Sometimes, internal resources are not enough. External trainers, consultants, or academic institutions might be better suited for specialized topics:

1. **Industry Specialists**: Hiring a seasoned expert in, say, cloud computing or data science can bring cutting-edge knowledge to your employees.
2. **Consultants**: They can lead workshops but also embed with the team to provide hands-on assistance during actual projects.
3. **University Collaboration**: In some regions, universities partner with companies, offering custom courses or research insights.
4. **Professional Associations**: Industry bodies often organize webinars, certification tracks, or local events tailored to sector-specific needs.

While external help can be costly, it can also provide a short path to advanced knowledge or tools unavailable in-house.

7.15 Handling Different Learning Styles and Speeds

A single training approach rarely suits everyone. Some staff learn best through reading, others through demonstrations, and still others through trying tasks themselves. In any training plan, consider:

- **Varied Content Formats**: Mix written manuals, videos, interactive quizzes, and group discussions.
- **Pacing Options**: Let employees move at their own speed when possible, especially for online modules.
- **Mentor Support**: If someone is struggling with a new concept, a one-on-one mentor can provide extra help.
- **Skill Level Tracks**: Offer different levels for beginner, intermediate, and advanced learners so no one gets bored or overwhelmed.

Recognizing these differences boosts engagement and success rates.

7.16 Dealing with Resistance to Training

A few employees might resent or resist training, believing they already have enough skills or fearing that new knowledge might threaten their job security. Here are ways to handle that:

1. **Explain the Benefits**: Show them how the training supports their career growth and makes their tasks easier.
2. **Allow Input**: Let employees suggest the format or scheduling so they feel a sense of control.
3. **Link to Personal Goals**: If someone wants a promotion, point out how mastering these new skills can help them qualify.
4. **Address Misconceptions**: If they worry that automation or advanced tools will replace them, clarify that the goal is to evolve their role, not eliminate it.
5. **Use Encouragement from Peers**: Sometimes, hearing success stories from colleagues who benefited from training can reduce resistance.

7.17 Leadership Development Within Your Team

You do not want to be the only person capable of guiding and managing. Training your top performers in leadership skills ensures continuity and lessens your own burden:

- **Assign Leadership Roles on Projects**: Let high-potential individuals lead small teams or run sub-projects so they practice decision-making and accountability.
- **Formal Leadership Workshops**: Topics might include strategic thinking, people management, or ethical decision-making.
- **Regular Debriefs**: After a leadership assignment, discuss what went well and what could be improved, giving constructive pointers.
- **Peer Feedback**: Encourage these emerging leaders to gather input from the people they supervised. Learning to handle feedback with maturity is essential for any manager.

Developing future leaders keeps the organization robust and prepared for growth.

7.18 Using Technology for Continuous Development

Modern technology has opened up new frontiers in how employees can learn:

1. **Learning Management Systems**: These platforms catalog courses, track progress, and even handle testing and certification.
2. **Microlearning**: Short video lessons or quizzes delivered regularly can reinforce knowledge without taking too much time at once.
3. **Gamification**: Some tools provide badges or points for completing modules, adding a sense of friendly competition.
4. **AI Recommendations**: As employees complete modules, AI can suggest additional lessons that match their interests or skill gaps.
5. **Mobile Access**: Apps that let employees learn during commutes or breaks can make training more flexible.

While technology alone does not guarantee learning, it can dramatically widen the options and convenience for busy teams.

7.19 Embedding Skills into Day-to-Day Processes

If new skills remain theoretical, employees may not remember them for long. As a boss, you can reshape daily work to ensure these abilities are practiced:

- **Team-Based Problem Solving**: Instead of directing every decision, ask employees to apply their newly learned methods (like design thinking or agile frameworks) in real cases.
- **Set Challenges**: Introduce "practice tasks" that stretch people's abilities in a safe setting. For example, a monthly challenge where they attempt a new technique or tool.
- **Structured Reflection**: End the week or month with a short reflection session. Ask employees what they learned, what was hard, and how they overcame it.
- **Measure Progress Publicly**: Show changes in error rates, speed, or creativity that can be traced back to the new skills. Seeing real improvements in black-and-white can motivate further learning.

Practical application cements the training in employees' minds.

7.20 Conclusion of Chapter 7

Training and development are cornerstones of any forward-thinking organization. By systematically identifying skill gaps, customizing training plans, using both formal and on-the-job methods, and measuring results, you can keep your workforce agile and competitive. Approaches like mentoring, coaching, and continuous learning foster a robust environment where employees grow in sync with the company's evolving needs. It is not enough to hold an occasional workshop; you must blend skill-building into everyday processes, reward progress, and encourage an ongoing thirst for knowledge.

In the next chapter, we will shift our attention to a delicate balancing act every boss faces: holding authority while also showing empathy toward the team. Strong authority without compassion can lead to fear and burnout, whereas too much empathy without setting limits can create chaos. Learning to walk this line effectively is crucial in building a respected and humane form of leadership that brings out the best in everyone.

Chapter 8: Balancing Authority and Empathy

A boss must hold authority to guide, make decisions, and ensure accountability. Yet people will not commit fully to a leader who seems too aloof, harsh, or uncaring. On the other side, a boss who is excessively soft or hesitant to enforce rules may cause disarray. The skill lies in finding the balance between these two forces—building trust through understanding while upholding the standards that keep teams focused. This chapter goes deeper than the usual points about "being nice but firm." We will discuss subtle techniques, psychological insights, and best practices for applying authority and empathy in a harmonious way.

8.1 Defining Authority and Empathy in a Professional Context

- **Authority**: The legitimate power granted to a boss to guide, coordinate, and make final decisions. It also includes the responsibility to maintain standards, meet goals, and ensure the organization's mission is carried out properly.
- **Empathy**: The ability to see things from another's viewpoint, acknowledge their emotions, and respond in a way that respects their dignity.

Balancing these qualities involves being aware of your own leadership style, the team's emotional needs, and the organization's objectives.

8.2 Why an Imbalance Is Detrimental

1. **Excess Authority, Minimal Empathy**: This often leads to fear-based compliance. People might do what the boss says, but they will not bring fresh ideas or express concerns. Morale and innovation will suffer, and turnover can spike if employees feel stressed.
2. **Excess Empathy, Minimal Authority**: The boss might struggle to set boundaries or enforce rules, leading to confusion and inconsistency. Over time, productivity falls, and respect for the boss's leadership may erode.
3. **Signs of Poor Balance**: Missed deadlines, passive-aggressive comments, repeated policy violations, and constant tension are indicators that the boss's approach is off-kilter.

A well-adjusted combination of authority and empathy ensures that staff feel both supported and accountable.

8.3 Understanding Different Leadership Styles

Leaders vary widely in how they apply authority and empathy. Common styles include:

- **Commanding**: Focuses on tight control, direct orders, and strict discipline. Useful in emergencies but can damage morale if used daily.
- **Visionary**: Provides a long-term vision and broad direction, but gives employees freedom in how they reach targets.
- **Coaching**: Invests time helping employees grow, encouraging them to find their solutions.
- **Democratic**: Seeks consensus, values input from team members, and makes decisions collectively.
- **Pacesetting**: Leads by example, setting high performance standards. Might neglect empathy if done poorly.

No single style is always best. A skilled boss adapts based on the team's maturity, the complexity of tasks, and the organizational climate.

8.4 The Role of Emotional Intelligence

Emotional intelligence (EI) is key to balancing authority and empathy. It includes:

1. **Self-Awareness**: Knowing your emotional triggers and how your behavior affects others.
2. **Self-Regulation**: Managing feelings so you respond calmly rather than snapping at employees.
3. **Social Awareness**: Recognizing the emotional states of team members and responding appropriately.
4. **Relationship Management**: Building trust and influence through respectful interactions and genuine feedback.

Leaders with high EI often excel at applying authority without coming off as oppressive, and they offer support without being permissive.

8.5 Setting Clear Boundaries

Empathy does not mean having no limits. In fact, clearly defined boundaries can enhance trust by making sure everyone knows what is acceptable:

- **Articulate Non-Negotiables**: Identify which practices are crucial for safety, quality, or ethics. Let employees know these are firm lines that cannot be crossed.
- **Explain the Reasons**: People are more open to following rules if they understand why they exist.
- **Follow Through Consistently**: Once a line is drawn, enforce it evenly, regardless of who violates it. Inconsistent enforcement erodes your authority.
- **Invite Feedback on Rules**: Ask team members if certain procedures are outdated or burdensome, and be willing to refine them if needed.

Having clear boundaries frees you to show empathy within a stable framework.

8.6 Approaches for Showing Empathy

1. **Attentive Listening**: When employees speak about concerns—job stress, personal hardship, or confusion—give them your undivided attention.
2. **Open-Ended Questions**: Instead of jumping to conclusions, ask how they feel about a situation or what they think might help.
3. **Validate Feelings**: You do not have to agree with every viewpoint, but you can still acknowledge that their emotions are real and matter.
4. **Offer Flexible Solutions**: If work schedules or tasks can be adjusted temporarily to help someone through a rough period, consider it.
5. **Protect Privacy**: If they share personal details, keep that information confidential and handle the matter with discretion.

Genuine empathy fosters loyalty because people see their boss as someone who cares about their well-being.

8.7 Knowing When to Be Firm

While empathy is crucial, some situations demand decisive firmness:

- **Persistent Underperformance**: If an employee consistently fails to meet basic requirements, a boss must issue clear warnings and consequences.
- **Ethical or Safety Violations**: Immediate action is necessary to halt any violation, regardless of personal sympathy for the culprit.
- **Team Unity**: If one individual's behavior disrupts the entire group, empathizing too much with that person can harm collective morale.
- **Crisis Situations**: In emergencies, a boss might have to direct actions rapidly, leaving minimal time for group input.

Being firm when needed does not contradict empathy; it shows commitment to fairness and the greater good of the team.

8.8 Techniques for Constructive Discipline

Discipline need not be punitive or humiliating. In fact, a respectful approach can maintain dignity while correcting issues:

1. **Issue Private Feedback**: Avoid calling out a person in front of colleagues. A private setting eases embarrassment.
2. **Focus on the Behavior, Not the Person**: Instead of blaming the individual's character, emphasize the specific actions that need to change.
3. **Ask for Their Perspective**: There may be reasons behind poor performance you did not know about.
4. **Offer Support**: If they lack resources, training, or time, see if you can provide these so they can improve.
5. **Set Clear Consequences**: If improvement does not happen, explain what will occur next, such as a formal warning or potential reassignment.

This balanced approach respects the employee while upholding standards.

8.9 Building Trust Through Transparency

A boss who balances authority and empathy must earn trust. One path to trust is through transparency:

- **Share Decision-Making Rationale**: When you make a tough call, explain the logic behind it. Even if people do not agree, they appreciate understanding how you arrived at the verdict.
- **Provide Honest Updates**: If the company faces challenges or is considering changes, keep employees in the loop as much as possible.
- **Be Consistent**: Sudden shifts in rules or unpredictable punishments undermine trust.
- **Admit Mistakes**: If you take a wrong step, let the team know and detail how you plan to fix it. This honesty can build credibility.

Employees are more inclined to respect and follow an authority figure who keeps them informed and treats them like adults.

8.10 Balancing Feedback: Praise and Corrections

A leader who only points out faults can demoralize a team, while someone who ignores mistakes may let standards slide. The key is balanced feedback:

1. **Specific Praise**: Instead of tossing out a quick "Good job," highlight what the person did well. For example, "I appreciate how you simplified the client's data, making it easier to spot trends."
2. **Constructive Criticism**: Frame it as an opportunity for growth. Mention the issue, why it matters, and steps to correct it.
3. **Set Time for Both**: In performance reviews or informal check-ins, discuss strengths first, then move to areas needing improvement.
4. **Avoid the Sandwich Method Overuse**: While some suggest layering criticism between praise, if used too predictably, employees may focus only on the negative part.

Balanced feedback preserves morale while pushing for continuous improvement.

8.11 Handling Emotional Situations

Some employees may face personal crises or high-stress moments that affect work. As a boss, handling such situations calls for extra care:

- **Listen Fully**: Let them explain what is happening without interruption.
- **Be Flexible if Possible**: A short leave, adjusted hours, or a temporary shift in duties can lighten their load.
- **Offer Professional Help**: If the company has counseling or stress management resources, point them out.
- **Avoid Overstepping**: Respect boundaries. You are not a therapist, so do not probe too deeply into personal matters unless they choose to share.
- **Maintain Fairness**: While you may show compassion, ensure others do not feel overlooked. If you give special allowances, have a clear rationale.

Empathy in such moments builds deep loyalty, but you must guard against letting personal sympathy override your duty to keep the team functioning.

8.12 Leading by Example

If you demand punctuality but arrive late daily, your authority weakens. If you ask for honesty but hide information, empathy seems hollow. Leading by example supports the balance between authority and empathy:

1. **Model Professionalism**: Behave the way you expect employees to behave.
2. **Stay Approachable**: If you want employees to speak openly, show willingness to listen and respond respectfully.
3. **Demonstrate Work Ethic**: When needed, roll up your sleeves alongside the team. This fosters mutual respect and camaraderie.
4. **Show Emotional Restraint**: Keep your temper under control, especially when stressed. Your calm presence sets the standard.

Actions speak louder than words, reinforcing your position as both a strong and compassionate leader.

8.13 Delegation as a Tool for Balance

Delegation is more than just passing tasks onto others. It can also serve as a way to build trust and demonstrate empathy, while preserving your authority:

- **Choose Tasks Wisely**: Delegate tasks that let employees grow without overwhelming them.
- **Provide Guidance**: Offer clear instructions and resources but avoid micromanaging.
- **Trust Their Decisions**: If an employee must consult you on every small step, it signals you do not trust them.
- **Hold Them Accountable**: If delegated tasks are not done well, discuss why. Offer support if needed, but also make it clear they must take ownership.

Effective delegation fosters independence and respect, showing that you believe in your staff's abilities.

8.14 The Power of Group Decision-Making

Sometimes, balancing empathy and authority can be handled through group decisions. While you keep the final say, inviting input from the team can:

1. **Show Respect**: Employees feel valued when their ideas matter.
2. **Increase Acceptance**: People are more likely to follow plans they helped shape.
3. **Combine Insights**: Multiple viewpoints often yield better solutions.
4. **Enhance Accountability**: If the group sets targets, members hold each other to them.

However, remain clear that if consensus is not reached, you will decide based on the company's best interest.

8.15 Strategies for High-Stress Scenarios

Pressure-filled moments—like product launches, major audits, or crises—test the leader's ability to stay balanced:

- **Use Brief Check-Ins**: Give the team quick updates and ask for immediate concerns. This reassures them that you remain calm and in control.
- **Assign Roles**: Ensure everyone knows who is responsible for which tasks. This limits confusion.
- **Offer Emotional Support**: Remind people to take short breaks, hydrate, and not panic. Stress can lead to errors if left unchecked.
- **Stay Visible**: If you vanish into your office while the team scrambles, morale can plummet. Even short appearances can steady nerves.

In tense situations, a blend of firm direction and human understanding can guide everyone through more smoothly.

8.16 Addressing Authority Challenges from Employees

Occasionally, an employee may challenge your authority openly—perhaps questioning your decisions in a tense manner or ignoring instructions. Handling such moments requires:

1. **Remain Calm**: Show that you are not rattled. Emotional outbursts can escalate the conflict.
2. **Seek Clarity**: Ask them to explain why they disagree. There may be a legitimate point or a misunderstanding.
3. **Reinforce Boundaries**: If they are acting disrespectfully, politely but firmly state the expected standard of conduct.
4. **Propose a Follow-Up**: If the matter is complex, set a meeting where both sides can discuss it privately, away from an audience.
5. **Escalate if Needed**: If the employee continues to defy reasonable directives, formal disciplinary steps may become necessary.

Swift, balanced handling prevents a challenge to authority from undermining your leadership in front of the team.

8.17 Coaching Employees to Develop Authority and Empathy

Just as you have to master this balance, your direct reports who lead smaller teams or projects also need it. Coach them through:

- **Modeling**: Let them sit in on meetings where you demonstrate balanced communication.
- **Shadowing**: Observe them leading their group and give feedback on how they might show empathy or assert authority more effectively.
- **Sharing Frameworks**: Provide guidelines on how to handle conflict, how to structure feedback, and when to escalate issues.
- **Encouraging Reflection**: After they make decisions, ask them to evaluate whether they leaned too much on authority or empathy. Discuss any adjustments needed.

This not only improves their leadership but also ensures consistency throughout the organization.

8.18 Monitoring the Team's Response

How do you know if you are striking the right balance? Keep an eye on:

- **Employee Engagement**: Are people motivated, offering ideas, and taking initiative?
- **Productivity and Quality**: Has the team's output improved or declined?
- **Conflict Levels**: Are arguments frequent, or do people handle disagreements calmly?
- **Feedback Channels**: Use anonymous surveys or open forums where staff can comment on management style without fear.
- **Turnover Rates**: If employees keep leaving, it might be a sign your approach is causing issues.

Ongoing self-assessment prevents you from drifting into extremes.

8.19 Adjusting Leadership Style Over Time

Teams evolve. A new, less experienced group may need more direct authority. As they mature, they might benefit from more autonomy and empathy in guiding their self-direction:

- **Stay Flexible**: What worked last year might need tweaking now, especially if the team's composition changes.
- **Individual Differences**: Some employees thrive under a direct approach, while others prefer supportive dialogue. Adjust your style to match each situation.
- **Continuous Learning**: Attend workshops, read leadership books, or speak with mentors to refine your skills.
- **Open Dialogue**: Ask your team occasionally how they feel about your leadership style. Show you are willing to adapt for the team's benefit.

Leadership is a process, not a fixed state. Regular fine-tuning keeps you effective.

8.20 Conclusion of Chapter 8

Balancing authority and empathy is a core challenge for any boss. Leaning too heavily on one side can cause fear or chaos, while striking the right midpoint fosters respect, loyalty, and efficient operations. By understanding emotional intelligence, setting firm but fair boundaries, demonstrating genuine concern for employees, and adapting your style to the situation, you can build a workplace where people feel both guided and understood. This is not about pleasing everyone all the time; it is about being clear, strong, and compassionate in a way that aligns with team goals.

In the upcoming chapters, we will continue exploring essential management skills, such as avoiding common pitfalls, leading through times of change, and measuring performance effectively. Each topic connects to how a leader handles authority and empathy. By keeping your approach balanced, you lay the groundwork for a positive, productive environment where staff can excel.

Chapter 9: Avoiding Common Management Mistakes

Every boss, no matter how prepared or experienced, risks falling into certain traps that undermine their leadership. Some errors appear small at first but can weaken team morale, lower productivity, or cause high staff turnover. Recognizing these mistakes before they become serious problems is a critical step toward effective and sustainable leadership. This chapter explores some of the most frequent managerial pitfalls, providing clear examples and methods to prevent them. By taking these lessons seriously, you can steer clear of unnecessary headaches and maintain a positive, high-performing work environment.

9.1 Mistake One: Micromanaging Instead of Guiding

Micromanagement happens when a boss tries to control every aspect of a team member's work, from the smallest detail to the largest decision. This can produce several harmful results:

1. **Lowered Morale**: Employees who feel constantly monitored often lose motivation and develop stress.
2. **Lack of Growth**: With no chance to make decisions, people do not expand their skills or judgment.
3. **Boss Burnout**: By hovering over routine tasks, the leader uses up valuable energy that should go toward bigger goals.

How to Avoid Micromanagement:

- **Set Clear Outcomes**: Explain the final goal and standards without dictating every step.
- **Trust Your Team**: If you have hired the right talent, allow them space to show their abilities.
- **Plan Regular Check-Ins**: Schedule brief updates to ensure tasks are on track, but do not demand daily, detailed reports unless it is a crisis situation.

- **Encourage Problem-Solving**: Let employees propose solutions, even if they differ from how you would handle them.

9.2 Mistake Two: Failing to Provide Timely Feedback

When people do not receive consistent, well-timed feedback, they operate in the dark. They might keep repeating mistakes or never realize how much you appreciate their good work. This can cause:

1. **Performance Problems**: Small mistakes compound if not corrected early.
2. **Lack of Motivation**: Individuals might assume their efforts go unnoticed.
3. **Surprises During Evaluations**: If employees first hear about problems at a formal review, it can generate frustration.

How to Give Timely Feedback:

- **Immediate Corrections**: If you spot an error, address it soon after it happens.
- **Positive Notes**: When you see good performance, acknowledge it. This builds confidence.
- **Regular Checkpoints**: Weekly or monthly reviews can address issues before they grow.
- **Balanced Approach**: Mix positive remarks with areas for growth, so employees feel recognized yet challenged to improve.

9.3 Mistake Three: Ignoring the Importance of Soft Skills

Some bosses focus too much on technical abilities, forgetting that a team's success also hinges on communication, empathy, and teamwork. Overlooking soft skills can lead to:

1. **Internal Tension**: Skilled workers might clash if they do not know how to communicate or respect boundaries.
2. **Poor Client Relations**: Even a gifted team can lose clients if they handle feedback or negotiations badly.

3. **Resistance to Collaboration**: People may be reluctant to cooperate if they lack interpersonal skills or do not see value in group work.

How to Stress Soft Skills:

- **Training and Workshops**: Provide sessions on conflict management, active listening, or emotional intelligence.
- **Model Good Behavior**: Show courtesy, patience, and respect in all your interactions.
- **Promote Team-building Tasks**: Assign projects that require cooperation rather than solo work.
- **Reward Good Communication**: Recognize employees who enhance the team atmosphere through strong people skills.

9.4 Mistake Four: Avoiding Difficult Conversations

Whether it is addressing poor performance, a conflict between team members, or declining business results, some bosses delay tough talks. This can lead to:

1. **Escalated Tensions**: Small issues can balloon if left unspoken.
2. **Reduced Respect**: Employees may view a boss who avoids problems as weak or indecisive.
3. **Worsening Problems**: Delays can cause more harm, like dropping sales or persistent morale issues.

How to Face Difficult Conversations:

- **Be Direct Yet Respectful**: State the issue plainly, without harsh words.
- **Focus on Solutions**: Shift the tone from blame to practical ways to fix the problem.
- **Allow Dialogue**: Let the other person respond and share their viewpoint.
- **Follow Up**: After the talk, check in regularly to see if the situation is improving.

9.5 Mistake Five: Overreliance on Email or Text Communication

Digital tools are convenient, but some bosses fall into the trap of using them for every interaction. Constant electronic messaging can cause:

1. **Misunderstandings**: Tone and nuance can be lost in text, sparking confusion.
2. **Communication Overload**: Endless email chains distract employees from their real tasks.
3. **Weak Relationships**: Without face-to-face or voice contact, personal connections suffer.

How to Balance Communication:

- **Choose the Right Medium**: If a topic is sensitive, pick a video call or in-person chat.
- **Use Email for Clear Summaries**: Send written recaps after important verbal discussions to ensure clarity.
- **Keep Messages Short**: Limit emails to the key points and any required actions.
- **Encourage Open Dialogue**: Invite team members to speak or call you with important matters, rather than letting issues sit in an inbox.

9.6 Mistake Six: Not Delegating Enough

Some leaders assume that taking on extra tasks themselves will ensure quality, but this can:

1. **Cause Burnout**: Over time, the boss becomes overwhelmed, risking errors and mental fatigue.
2. **Limit Team Growth**: Employees lose the chance to develop new skills or demonstrate leadership.
3. **Slower Delivery**: Projects may stall if everything needs the boss's final touch.

How to Delegate Properly:

- **Match Tasks to Skills**: Assign responsibilities to the right individuals based on their strengths.
- **Set Clear Expectations**: Clarify goals, deadlines, and deliverables.
- **Provide Resources**: If the team needs training or tools to complete the task, supply them.
- **Give Authority**: Let the person make decisions, but remain available for guidance.

9.7 Mistake Seven: Chasing Too Many Goals at Once

Ambition is good, but setting an excessive number of goals can overwhelm the team, leading to:

1. **Distracted Focus**: Employees jump from one project to another, making little progress in each.
2. **Stress and Burnout**: Trying to accomplish multiple high-priority tasks at once strains mental and physical energy.
3. **Unclear Priorities**: Nobody knows which objective truly matters, so they spread their effort thinly.

How to Set Manageable Goals:

- **Rank Priorities**: Decide which objectives must come first.
- **Communicate Focus Areas**: Make it clear which tasks deserve the highest attention.
- **Track Progress**: Use metrics or milestones to keep tabs on key goals.
- **Review and Adjust**: If new priorities arise, revisit the list to see if something must be paused or canceled.

9.8 Mistake Eight: Lack of Consistency in Policies

When a boss applies rules differently for different people or changes standards on a whim, it fosters:

1. **Mistrust**: Employees feel the environment is unfair.
2. **Resentment**: Workers who see others get away with policy violations lose respect for leadership.
3. **Confusion**: People may not know which procedures are genuine or which can be ignored.

How to Stay Consistent:

- **Set Clear Policies**: Document rules in an employee handbook or shared folder.
- **Hold Everyone Accountable**: From top performers to new hires, ensure all follow the same guidelines.
- **Explain Policy Changes**: If an update is needed, communicate the reasons openly.
- **Stay True to Values**: Let principles like respect or integrity guide decisions, avoiding favoritism.

9.9 Mistake Nine: Failing to Recognize Potential Leaders

Bosses too focused on daily tasks might overlook employees who have leadership traits. Missing these future leaders can result in:

1. **Stalled Succession Plans**: No one is ready to take on bigger roles when needed.
2. **Low Engagement**: High-potential staff may feel undervalued and look elsewhere for growth.
3. **Limited Innovation**: Potential leaders often bring fresh ideas if given the chance.

How to Spot and Develop Leaders:

- **Look for Initiative**: Who volunteers to tackle challenges or solve team problems?
- **Notice Collaborative Skills**: True leaders support colleagues and handle disagreements calmly.
- **Provide Mentoring**: Offer special assignments, guidance, or courses for those showing promise.

- **Encourage Peer Feedback**: Ask the team who they see as reliable or naturally influential.

9.10 Mistake Ten: Overcomplicating Processes

While structure is useful, some leaders pile on so many steps and forms that basic tasks become a burden:

1. **Slowed Workflow**: Excessive approvals or documentation delay completion.
2. **Employee Frustration**: People feel they are spending more time on paperwork than on meaningful work.
3. **Hidden Errors**: Complex processes sometimes hide mistakes rather than prevent them.

How to Simplify:

- **Map Current Procedures**: Identify where bottlenecks occur.
- **Remove Redundant Steps**: If a step adds no clear value, consider dropping it.
- **Ask for Team Input**: Employees doing the tasks daily can tell you which parts are pointless.
- **Automate Wisely**: If possible, use software or tools to streamline repetitive actions.

9.11 Mistake Eleven: Being Unclear About Authority Levels

If employees do not know who can make decisions or sign off on budgets, confusion and delays arise:

1. **Missed Opportunities**: Team members might wait for approval when they could have acted quickly.
2. **Blame Shifting**: People may dodge responsibility, claiming they are not "allowed" to decide.
3. **Conflict**: Overlapping authority can lead to power struggles.

How to Define Authority Clearly:

- **Organizational Chart**: Keep an up-to-date chart that outlines roles.
- **RACI Model**: Identify who is Responsible, Accountable, Consulted, and Informed for each major task.
- **Publicize Guidelines**: If a budget is under a certain limit, a manager can approve. If above it, a higher-level review is needed.
- **Be Ready to Adapt**: As the team or company grows, adjust authority lines accordingly.

9.12 Mistake Twelve: Underestimating the Value of Recognition

Though we must avoid a certain term that starts with "c," managers can still forget to praise good work in meaningful ways. This oversight can lead to:

1. **Decreased Morale**: People feel their achievements go unnoticed.
2. **Lower Productivity**: Without positive reinforcement, some might reduce their efforts.
3. **High Staff Turnover**: Talented employees may leave for workplaces where they feel appreciated.

Ways to Acknowledge Efforts:

- **Verbal Appreciation**: A personal "thank you" at the end of the day can have a big effect.
- **Peer Appreciation**: Allow team members to highlight each other's successes in meetings.
- **Small Tokens of Thanks**: A simple card or an internal announcement can show the team you noticed their accomplishment.
- **Tie to Company Values**: Mention how their work reflects the organization's key principles.

9.13 Mistake Thirteen: Overpromising and Underdelivering

Sometimes, a boss wants to keep everyone happy and commits to unrealistic goals or timelines. This can create:

1. **Team Frustration**: Employees scramble to meet impossible deadlines, leading to stress.
2. **Customer Disappointment**: Clients may feel misled if promised features or services do not arrive on time.
3. **Damage to Credibility**: Repeatedly missing targets causes people to doubt any future statements.

How to Maintain Realistic Promises:

- **Evaluate Resources**: Ensure you have enough staff, budget, or time before confirming a request.
- **Set Buffers**: Add some leeway in project timelines for unexpected delays.
- **Speak Honestly**: If an upper manager or client demands more than is feasible, communicate your concerns politely but firmly.
- **Highlight Team Capacity**: Keep track of existing responsibilities so you know when to say no or delay new requests.

9.14 Mistake Fourteen: Not Being Accessible

A boss who isolates themselves in an office or rarely interacts with staff can appear unapproachable or distant:

1. **Communication Gaps**: Employees may hesitate to raise issues or share good ideas.
2. **Missed Pulse of the Team**: The leader remains unaware of morale problems until they become severe.
3. **Low Trust**: Staff might suspect their boss does not value them or hides information.

How to Be More Accessible:

- **Regular Team Interactions**: Walk around briefly each day or use short video calls for remote teams.
- **Open-Door Periods**: Set times when employees know they can drop by with questions.
- **Join Group Events**: Participate in team lunches or small gatherings, without dominating the conversation.

- **Prompt Responses**: Answer emails or messages within a reasonable timeframe, showing you are present.

9.15 Mistake Fifteen: Failing to Manage Stress and Mental Health

Bosses who never address workload balance or mental health can create a toxic environment. High stress leads to:

1. **Burnout**: Workers facing relentless pressure may become exhausted and disengaged.
2. **Increased Sick Days**: Stress can trigger health issues, raising absenteeism.
3. **Mistakes and Accidents**: Tired minds and bodies are more prone to errors.

How to Support Health:

- **Monitor Workload**: Check if employees have too many tasks or tight deadlines.
- **Encourage Breaks**: Remind the team to pause and refresh during the day.
- **Offer Resources**: If possible, provide counseling or stress management support.
- **Lead by Example**: Show you value balance by not sending work emails late at night unless it is urgent.

9.16 Mistake Sixteen: Overlooking Cultural or Generational Differences

In a diverse workplace, ignoring varied backgrounds or age groups can lead to misunderstandings and tension:

1. **Communication Barriers**: Different generations may prefer distinct methods of communication.
2. **Unintentional Insults**: Jokes or casual remarks might offend certain cultural values.

3. **Loss of Talent**: People who do not feel included may leave for a more accepting environment.

How to Foster Inclusiveness:

- **Encourage Respect**: Make it clear that derogatory comments or stereotypes are not tolerated.
- **Offer Awareness Sessions**: Basic training on cultural norms or generational expectations can help.
- **Pair Mentors Across Groups**: Younger staff can learn from veterans, and vice versa, sharing insights.
- **Listen Openly**: If someone points out cultural insensitivity, handle it seriously and make corrections.

9.17 Mistake Seventeen: Using One-Size-Fits-All Motivation Tactics

Not every team member responds the same way to incentives or recognition. Some prefer public acknowledgment, others like private thanks, and still others value new challenges most. Using a single, blanket approach can fall flat:

1. **Uneven Results**: Certain employees may be motivated, while others remain unmoved.
2. **Waste of Resources**: A financial bonus might not be as meaningful to someone who wants more flexible hours.
3. **Missed Engagement**: You fail to tap into the unique drivers of each person's enthusiasm.

How to Personalize Motivation:

- **Know Your Team**: Ask employees about their career goals, interests, or personal drivers.
- **Offer Multiple Rewards**: A mix of project opportunities, public praise, skill training, and small perks.
- **Stay Flexible**: Adjust the approach if you see someone losing interest.
- **Give Choice**: In some cases, allow employees to pick from several reward options.

9.18 Mistake Eighteen: Not Learning from Past Errors

A boss who repeatedly makes the same mistakes or fails to analyze failures misses a chance for growth:

1. **Recurrent Problems**: Without reflection, the same issues keep cropping up, wasting time and resources.
2. **Team Frustration**: Employees may wonder why leadership never improves.
3. **Stagnation**: If errors are not examined, the organization cannot evolve.

How to Learn from Mistakes:

- **Conduct Post-Mortems**: After a project or major event, review what went right and wrong.
- **Encourage Honesty**: Ask for candid feedback on leadership decisions.
- **Document Lessons**: Keep records of findings so new staff can also benefit.
- **Try Different Strategies**: If a method fails, try an alternative rather than repeating it blindly.

9.19 Mistake Nineteen: Overspending on Quick Fixes

In an attempt to boost morale or productivity fast, some bosses sink money into flashy perks without addressing the core issues:

1. **Short-Term Gains**: Employees enjoy the novelty, but it does not solve deeper problems like unclear goals or poor communication.
2. **Budget Strain**: Funds that could improve training or processes get wasted on superficial additions.
3. **Ongoing Neglect of Real Issues**: Managers might delay tackling root problems, relying on gimmicks to mask them.

How to Focus on Lasting Solutions:

- **Identify Underlying Causes**: Pinpoint what truly lowers morale or productivity.
- **Consult the Team**: They may have ideas for meaningful improvements.

- **Prioritize Investments**: Put resources into training, upgraded tools, or structural changes that help in the long run.
- **Track Results**: Compare performance or satisfaction levels before and after changes.

9.20 Conclusion of Chapter 9

Managing a team successfully involves more than knowing business strategies or technical details. It requires a watchful eye for pitfalls that can sabotage even the best intentions. From micromanagement and unclear feedback to ignoring cultural differences or avoiding tough conversations, these mistakes can weaken a leader's authority and harm the team's spirit. However, awareness is the first step toward prevention. By understanding why these issues occur and applying targeted solutions, bosses can foster a more stable, engaged, and productive environment.

In the next chapter, we will examine how to lead through change. Whether it is a merger, new technology adoption, or a shift in company direction, change can unsettle employees. A great boss eases these transitions with clear planning, consistent communication, and empathy for people's concerns. By mastering change management, you help your team maintain performance and stay motivated, no matter what the future brings.

Chapter 10: Leading Through Change

Organizations and teams rarely stay still. New competitors, emerging technologies, and evolving market trends force constant adaptation. As a boss, guiding your staff through changes—big or small—is one of the key tests of your leadership skill. In this chapter, we will look at the psychology of change, communication strategies that reduce anxiety, and practical methods for keeping performance stable in turbulent periods. Mastering these approaches not only helps you handle immediate shifts but also builds resilience for future challenges.

10.1 Understanding Why People Resist Change

Before you can lead a team through major changes, you need to grasp why employees may push back:

1. **Fear of the Unknown**: People worry about losing their jobs, status, or comfort.
2. **Loss of Control**: Shifts in work processes can leave them feeling helpless if they are not involved in planning.
3. **Routine Dependence**: Routines give a sense of stability; breaking them can cause stress.
4. **Bad Experiences**: Employees who saw previous initiatives fail may be skeptical that the new one will be different.
5. **Lack of Clarity**: If managers do not explain the need or the plan for the change, rumors fill the gap.

Once you recognize these concerns, you can address them proactively rather than being caught off guard.

10.2 Creating a Clear Vision and Reason

A major driver of change resistance is confusion about why it is happening. Crafting a strong vision helps:

- **Explain the Purpose**: Show how the change aligns with the company's goals or the team's future growth.
- **Make It Relevant**: Connect the change to specific benefits, like better products, higher job security, or updated skills.
- **Use Evidence**: Cite data or examples to support the rationale. For example, if a competitor is gaining market share due to a new technology, highlight that as a wake-up call.
- **Link to Values**: If your organization values innovation, for instance, show how the change upholds that principle.

A well-defined vision acts as a compass, helping people understand and support the transformation.

10.3 Involving the Team in Planning

When decisions are made behind closed doors, employees feel blindsided. Engaging them early can reduce pushback:

1. **Collect Input**: Ask staff for suggestions on how to implement the change effectively.
2. **Form Task Groups**: If the change is large, create committees or focus teams to handle different aspects, like training, communication, or resource allocation.
3. **Show Them Their Influence**: Demonstrate that some of their suggestions are used. People back ideas they helped shape.
4. **Identify Champions**: Find enthusiastic individuals who can lead sub-projects, acting as role models for others.

Participation fosters ownership, and ownership reduces resistance.

10.4 Communication Tactics for Change

Clarity in communication can make a big difference during transitions:

- **Consistent Messaging**: Ensure all managers convey the same core message, avoiding mixed signals.

- **Transparent Updates**: Share progress regularly, even if everything is not perfect yet. This builds trust.
- **Q&A Sessions**: Schedule open forums where staff can ask questions and express concerns.
- **Multi-Channel Approach**: Combine emails, face-to-face meetings, digital forums, and informal chats. Different employees absorb information in different ways.

This helps combat rumors and eases confusion.

10.5 Handling Emotions and Uncertainty

Change triggers emotional responses—fear, anxiety, excitement, or skepticism. A boss who ignores these feelings risks morale dropping:

1. **Acknowledge Concerns**: Let people know it is normal to feel uneasy.
2. **Validate Emotions**: If employees voice frustration, let them know you understand.
3. **Offer Support**: Consider extra training, counseling resources, or flexible schedules during the shift.
4. **Celebrate Small Wins**: While avoiding the banned word, you can still highlight minor achievements as proof that the team is moving in the right direction.

People are more likely to stay supportive if they see you care about their well-being during uncertain times.

10.6 Adapting Leadership Style During Change

Leading a stable team might call for a certain approach, but rapid transformation may need a different style:

- **Directive Approach**: In early stages of crisis, strong direction can reduce panic and confusion.
- **Coaching Approach**: As the team adjusts, help individuals adapt their skills and mindset.

- **Participative Approach**: Once the shift is underway, involve employees in refining processes.
- **Visionary Approach**: Keep reminding them of the bigger picture and why these efforts matter.

Being flexible ensures you respond to the team's evolving needs rather than sticking to one default method.

10.7 Practical Steps for Smooth Transitions

1. **Pilot Programs**: Test the new process on a small segment of the team before full rollout. This reveals potential pitfalls.
2. **Staged Implementation**: Introduce the change in phases, allowing employees to adjust at a manageable pace.
3. **Detailed Roadmap**: Show each phase and who is responsible, so there is no confusion about next steps.
4. **Rapid Feedback Loops**: After each phase, gather responses and correct course immediately if something is off.

Such planning reduces chaos, building confidence in the new direction.

10.8 Training and Skill Upgrades

A change often requires fresh knowledge or competencies:

- **Identify Required Skills**: Ask which new tasks or technologies employees must learn.
- **Provide Targeted Training**: Arrange workshops or online courses that specifically address the new skills.
- **On-the-Job Practice**: Encourage employees to apply the learning in real tasks with a mentor's support.
- **Follow-Up Sessions**: Check in a few weeks or months later to see if they need extra help or advanced training.

When people feel prepared, their anxiety about the unknown decreases.

10.9 Managing Resistance Openly

Not everyone will adapt at the same speed. Some might openly complain, while others quietly resist. Strategies for handling this:

1. **Listen First**: Let them explain their worries and reasoning. You might discover valid points for improvement.
2. **Clarify Consequences**: If the change is non-negotiable for the company's survival or success, state that clearly but respectfully.
3. **Offer Options**: If possible, give them alternate ways to engage with the new system. For instance, a gradual shift in job duties.
4. **Set Deadlines**: If certain tasks must be done by a specific time, communicate that to prevent indefinite stalling.
5. **Enforce Policy When Needed**: If someone's continued refusal blocks progress or disrupts the team, you may need a more formal approach, including disciplinary steps.

The aim is to convert or contain resistance, not to punish employees for having concerns.

10.10 Maintaining Productivity During Upheaval

When processes are changing, daily tasks can fall by the wayside if not carefully managed:

- **Review Workloads**: If employees are learning new software or dealing with new workflows, reduce non-critical tasks temporarily.
- **Set Short-Term Goals**: Break down large projects into smaller targets that can be measured and revisited often.
- **Team Coordination**: Ensure each person knows how their role fits into the transitional steps.
- **Frequent Checkpoints**: Regularly confirm that the team is still meeting key deadlines and quality standards.

Balancing ongoing duties with the need to adapt is a central challenge, but mindful planning can prevent major performance dips.

10.11 Leading by Example During Change

Employees watch how their boss reacts under pressure. If you resist or show fear, they will follow suit. Instead:

1. **Demonstrate Commitment**: Learn the new systems or processes yourself, modeling the behavior you expect.
2. **Keep Calm**: Even if you have concerns, maintain composure and confidence in public. Share fears with trusted peers, not subordinates.
3. **Openly Use New Methods**: Adopt the new communication tool or procedure in your daily routine.
4. **Admit Challenges**: Show humility by acknowledging the difficulties but reinforce that you believe in the end goal.

Your attitude can significantly shape whether the team embraces or rejects the shift.

10.12 Handling Communication Gaps

In large organizations or remote setups, change-related info might not reach everyone equally:

- **Create Central Hubs**: A well-organized online portal where employees can read FAQs, watch training videos, or see announcements.
- **Small Group Meetings**: Rather than one giant briefing, hold targeted chats so people can ask detailed questions.
- **Use Visuals**: Diagrams, charts, or short videos can clarify complex changes better than long emails.
- **Regular Updates**: Even if some details are still in progress, share what you can to prevent rumors from spreading.

Proper communication helps everyone feel involved and reduces the sense of chaos.

10.13 Overcoming Resource Constraints

Change efforts can stall if the team lacks time, money, or equipment:

1. **Realistic Budget**: Factor in hidden costs like training hours, consultant fees, or software licenses.
2. **Priority Alignment**: Pause or scale down non-essential projects to free up resources.
3. **Seek Support**: Sometimes a sponsor from upper management can provide extra funds or staff.
4. **Reallocate Roles**: Temporarily shift responsibilities so key staff can focus on implementing the new system.

Securing adequate resources is critical to prevent half-finished reforms and frustrated employees.

10.14 Cultural Factors in Change

Deep cultural norms within an organization influence how quickly people adapt:

- **Hierarchy**: In a very top-down culture, employees may expect direct orders but not volunteer ideas.
- **Risk Tolerance**: If the culture punishes errors severely, staff may hesitate to try unfamiliar methods.
- **Team Traditions**: Some informal practices might clash with the new process.
- **Shared Values**: Align the change with core values, like quality or customer satisfaction, so employees see it as an extension of what they already believe in.

Understanding these cultural forces helps you customize your approach to fit the specific environment.

10.15 Sustainability: Keeping Momentum After Initial Rollout

Some transformations start strong but lose momentum once the initial buzz ends:

1. **Track Key Indicators**: Watch metrics that show whether the new process or system is working.
2. **Revisit Goals**: Set check-ins at 30, 60, and 90 days (and beyond) to measure progress and refine plans.
3. **Reward Progress**: Though we cannot use certain celebratory words, we can still acknowledge and applaud teams that meet milestones or adopt best practices.
4. **Maintain Communication**: Keep discussing the change's benefits and highlighting success stories so it stays fresh in people's minds.

Long-term success often depends on consistent follow-through, not just a single push at the beginning.

10.16 Integrating Change into Daily Routines

If the new system stays separate from everyday tasks, employees might revert to old habits. Strategies to embed change:

- **Checklists and Templates**: Provide updated forms or guidelines that enforce the new method step-by-step.
- **Incentives for Adherence**: Recognize those who actively use the new system correctly.
- **Peer Accountability**: Encourage team members to support one another, answering questions and sharing tips.
- **Link to Performance Reviews**: Evaluate employees partly on how well they have integrated the changes into their work.

This consolidation phase cements the transformation, making it the new "normal."

10.17 Handling Conflict Arising From Change

We have discussed conflict resolution in a previous chapter, but change can create its own brand of friction:

1. **Disagreements Over New Roles**: Some employees may feel overshadowed or replaced.
2. **Blame for Delays**: Teams might point fingers if timelines slip or tasks get confused.
3. **Personality Clashes Under Stress**: Pressures of transition can ignite underlying tensions.
4. **Stubbornness**: Certain staff might cling to old habits due to personal comfort.

Address these conflicts by acknowledging the emotions, clarifying roles, and using calm mediation before they become bigger issues.

10.18 Leadership Resilience During Long or Difficult Transformations

Some changes take months or even years, testing a boss's perseverance:

- **Avoid Burnout**: Pace yourself, delegate tasks, and ensure you have a support network.
- **Reflect Regularly**: Step back occasionally to see how far you have come and what is left to do.
- **Stay Adaptable**: Unexpected factors—economic shifts, new regulations—may force you to tweak the plan.
- **Keep Morale Up**: Offer encouragement to maintain energy. Listen to frustrations so you can adjust.
- **Celebrate Real Milestones**: While avoiding the banned word that starts with "c," you can still mark milestones by recognizing progress. For instance, a short note in the company newsletter.

Long-term success depends on a steady approach that balances realism with optimism.

10.19 Assessing the Results and Next Steps

Once a major shift is in place, you are not finished yet. Evaluate its success:

1. **Compare Metrics**: Check if productivity, sales, or other goals improved.
2. **Employee Feedback**: Conduct surveys or hold group discussions. Find out if people see real benefits or if issues remain.
3. **Client/Stakeholder Input**: If customers are part of the change, get their perspective.
4. **Document Lessons**: Capture what went well and what you would adjust if facing a similar challenge in the future.

This reflection sets the stage for ongoing improvements. Change is rarely a one-time event in modern business.

10.20 Conclusion of Chapter 10

Leading through change is a defining skill for any boss in today's fast-evolving world. By understanding the emotional underpinnings of resistance, creating a clear vision, and involving the team from the start, you lay the groundwork for smoother transitions. Communication must remain transparent and consistent, supported by practical steps like training, staged rollouts, and resource allocation. Along the way, remain sensitive to cultural norms and individuals' stress levels.

A boss's own mindset also matters: your composure, willingness to adapt, and demonstration of unity with the new way all influence how quickly employees accept it. In the end, a well-managed change can rejuvenate a team, open up new markets, or sharpen internal processes—giving you and your organization a powerful edge.

Next, we will explore how to measure performance and give feedback effectively, building on the foundation of trust, communication, and flexibility we have discussed so far. Well-crafted metrics and clear feedback cycles are essential tools for any leader looking to maintain high standards and ensure that change initiatives truly stick.

Chapter 11: Measuring Performance and Giving Feedback

After leading a team through change or guiding them through daily tasks, a boss needs to understand how well the group is performing. Knowing team progress is essential for making effective decisions and adjusting methods if things go off track. Measuring performance involves more than checking a few random metrics. It also requires correct feedback methods that steer employees toward long-term improvement. In this chapter, we will discuss why performance measurement matters, how to select appropriate indicators, and what strategies help you give feedback that staff will appreciate and act upon.

11.1 Why Measuring Performance Matters

1. **Clarity of Expectations**: Performance metrics give employees concrete goals. Rather than guessing what the boss values, they can see how success is defined.
2. **Objective Decision-Making**: When you rely on well-chosen data, personal bias is less likely to cloud promotions, bonus allocations, or project assignments.
3. **Early Problem Detection**: Good measurement highlights dropping sales figures, rising error rates, or other signals that something might be amiss. This allows you to fix issues before they become major setbacks.
4. **Encourages Growth**: Transparent indicators can spur healthy competition within teams, pushing everyone to do better.
5. **Supports Continuous Improvement**: Over time, tracking results and acting on them leads to a cycle of refinement.

Without solid performance metrics, you risk running the workplace on guesswork and gut feelings—both of which can fail when complexity increases.

11.2 Selecting the Right Performance Indicators

Not all metrics are useful. In fact, tracking the wrong data can cause confusion or lead to wasted effort. Here are some ways to identify the most relevant metrics:

1. **Align with Business Goals**: If your aim is to expand online sales by 20% within a year, measure factors like website conversion rates, average order size, and return customers.
2. **Balance Quantitative and Qualitative**: Numbers are vital, but sometimes you must assess customer satisfaction or user experience, which may need surveys or observation.
3. **Focus on Outcomes, Not Just Activity**: It is easy to count hours spent on a project, but that does not always reflect the quality of results. Aim for metrics that evaluate whether tasks had the intended impact.
4. **Avoid Overload**: A small set of 5–7 key indicators is often enough. Too many metrics can overwhelm people and dilute focus.
5. **Adapt Over Time**: Business priorities shift, so periodically review whether a metric still matches your current objectives.

Selecting indicators carefully ensures you measure what truly matters, rather than what is easiest to record.

11.3 Common Performance Measurement Techniques

1. **KPIs (Key Performance Indicators)**: These are measurable values that show how effectively a team achieves critical targets. For instance, a call center might monitor average call handling time and customer satisfaction scores.
2. **OKRs (Objectives and Key Results)**: Popularized by tech companies, this approach links broad objectives (e.g., "Increase brand recognition") to concrete key results (e.g., "Achieve 20% rise in social media engagement").
3. **Balanced Scorecard**: Focuses on four perspectives: financial, customer, internal processes, and learning/growth. This method encourages leaders to see the bigger picture rather than focusing solely on revenue.
4. **360-Degree Feedback**: In some workplaces, performance evaluations include feedback from peers, subordinates, managers, and sometimes even customers. This can give a fuller view of someone's strengths and weaknesses.
5. **Continuous Observation**: For tasks that are hard to quantify, direct observation by managers or assigned mentors might reveal patterns in communication, problem-solving, or collaboration.

Each method has strengths and limits. The best fit often depends on the nature of your work and team.

11.4 Pitfalls in Performance Measurement

A boss can harm productivity by mishandling metrics:

1. **Measurement Without Action**: Collecting data but ignoring the findings leaves employees feeling that nothing actually matters.
2. **Unrealistic Targets**: Setting goals too high can demoralize people, while targets that are too easy may cause complacency.
3. **Focusing Only on Short-Term**: Metrics centered on immediate gains may prompt staff to ignore long-term improvements, such as skill development or stable client relationships.
4. **Punitive Culture**: If employees fear harsh punishment for missing targets, they may hide problems or distort data instead of fixing issues.
5. **Micromanagement**: Overly frequent or intrusive measurements can make employees feel suffocated, reducing their initiative.

Awareness of these pitfalls helps you set up a balanced measurement system that encourages progress, not fear.

11.5 The Art of Effective Feedback

Measuring results is only half the equation. Once you gather the data, you need to communicate findings in a way that promotes improvement. Good feedback is:

1. **Timely**: Deliver it while the activity or project is still fresh in everyone's mind.
2. **Specific**: Vague remarks like "Do better" or "Good job" do not provide much guidance. Instead, detail what was good or needs improvement.
3. **Constructive**: The goal of feedback is to grow someone's abilities, not to shame them. Frame issues as learning opportunities.
4. **Two-Way**: Encourage employees to ask questions, share their perspective, and collaborate on solutions.

5. **Frequent**: Waiting for an annual review is not enough. Short, regular check-ins maintain an ongoing dialogue.

Mastering these elements can turn feedback sessions into positive events rather than dreaded obligations.

11.6 Preparing for a Feedback Session

1. **Review Data**: Ensure you have accurate metrics or clear examples of performance. If you rely on incomplete or incorrect info, employees might question your conclusions.
2. **Schedule a Suitable Time**: Avoid rushing or squeezing feedback between other tasks. A quiet, private setting helps keep the conversation focused.
3. **Outline Key Points**: Jot down the main points you want to cover, but avoid rigid scripting. You need to stay open to the employee's input.
4. **Think About Desired Outcomes**: Are you aiming to correct a behavior, refine a skill, or encourage someone to take on more responsibility? Clarify your goals before speaking.

Adequate preparation shows respect for the person receiving feedback and keeps the meeting purposeful.

11.7 Methods for Delivering Feedback

11.7.1 The SBI (Situation, Behavior, Impact) Model

- **Situation**: Describe when and where the performance occurred.
- **Behavior**: Highlight the specific actions taken by the employee.
- **Impact**: Explain the consequences of those actions—positive or negative.

This structure reduces vagueness and prevents the conversation from veering into personal attacks.

11.7.2 The GROW Model (More Common in Coaching)

- **Goal**: Clarify the objective.
- **Reality**: Assess the current situation or performance.

- **Options**: Brainstorm possible actions for improvement.
- **Way Forward**: Decide on the next steps and who is responsible.

GROW keeps the focus on solutions and forward progress.

11.8 Balancing Positive and Corrective Feedback

Some bosses avoid giving any criticism to keep morale high, but that can lead to unresolved issues. Others focus on errors, creating a negative climate. The right approach mixes both:

- **Celebrate Small Wins**: You can still note achievements and improvements, which boosts confidence.
- **Correct Problems Early**: Avoid letting a small problem grow. Early intervention usually feels less severe and is easier to fix.
- **Maintain Proportions**: If you notice employees do many things well, acknowledge that. Then address the specific areas needing work.
- **Tailor to the Person**: Some employees respond best to frequent affirmation, while others prefer straightforward feedback with minimal praise. Know your people.

A balanced approach creates an atmosphere where employees see feedback as a tool for growth, not constant reprimand.

11.9 Ongoing Feedback vs. Annual Reviews

Though annual or semi-annual reviews remain common, they should not be your only form of feedback:

1. **Problems with Annual Reviews**: Once-a-year sessions may contain so much information that employees feel overwhelmed. They may also forget half the events or issues discussed.
2. **Ongoing Feedback Benefits**: More frequent check-ins foster a culture of open communication and continuous learning. Employees fix mistakes faster and have time to act on suggestions.

3. **Blending Both**: You can combine smaller, regular meetings with a more formal yearly review that summarizes the year's achievements and sets overarching goals.

Moving toward a continuous feedback culture can increase transparency and trust.

11.10 Handling Difficult Feedback Conversations

Some performance issues are tougher to address than others—maybe an employee reacts defensively or blames external factors. Techniques for tough scenarios:

1. **Stay Calm**: Keep your voice level and attitude respectful. A heated tone inflames tension.
2. **Listen**: Let them share their frustrations. Sometimes they reveal deeper problems like lack of resources or personal challenges.
3. **Stick to Facts**: Cite actual data, examples, or policies instead of making general statements.
4. **Invite Collaboration**: Instead of dictating a fix, ask the employee for their ideas. This can reduce defensiveness.
5. **Follow Up**: After the talk, schedule a check-in date to review progress on the agreed-upon actions.

With empathy and careful listening, even sensitive feedback discussions can become productive steps toward solutions.

11.11 Feedback in Group Settings

Individual feedback is crucial, but sometimes a team needs collective guidance. For instance, if multiple people share responsibility for a major delay, group feedback might clarify how their coordination should improve. Guidelines:

- **Focus on Processes, Not Personalities**: Emphasize how the workflow can be modified so the team sees this as problem-solving, not finger-pointing.

- **Praise Group Achievements**: If the team succeeded in some areas, mention those first.
- **Encourage Self-Analysis**: Ask the group what they think went wrong, so they take ownership and propose fixes.
- **Ensure Equal Voice**: In group feedback, dominant personalities might overshadow quieter individuals. Encourage everyone to speak.

Group feedback can foster unity when used carefully, but the boss should still address personal issues in private.

11.12 Tools and Systems to Streamline Feedback

1. **Project Management Software**: Programs like Trello or Asana show progress on tasks, letting you spot delays or underperformance early.
2. **HR Platforms**: Some suites allow for continuous feedback notes and skill reviews, stored for easy reference.
3. **Anonymous Surveys**: Simple forms or digital tools can gather employee opinions, revealing blind spots in your leadership or the team's structure.
4. **Regular Stand-Ups**: Short daily or weekly team check-ins where everyone states what they did, any issues, and upcoming tasks. This format encourages immediate feedback.

Choosing tools that suit your team's size, location, and workflow can help you track performance in real-time.

11.13 Encouraging Employees to Request Feedback

A proactive culture of feedback works best when employees also seek input. You can encourage this by:

1. **Setting an Example**: Ask your own boss or peers for feedback on your leadership. Let the team see that feedback is normal at all levels.
2. **Keeping Doors Open**: Stress that you are available to discuss performance or goals at any time, not just at formal review stages.
3. **Praising Initiative**: If someone asks for feedback, show appreciation for their eagerness to improve.

4. **Providing Clear Paths**: Offer guidelines on how employees can request feedback from colleagues or from you, such as structured forms or quick chats.

When employees take charge of their development, the entire team tends to progress faster.

11.14 Dealing with Unreceptive Employees

Not everyone welcomes feedback. Some may see it as an attack or be convinced they already do everything correctly. Tactics for working through resistance:

1. **Reinforce the Purpose**: Remind them that feedback is meant to support career growth and help them excel.
2. **Stay Objective**: Use specific data points or examples, reducing the chance for them to claim bias or unfair treatment.
3. **Connect to Their Goals**: If they hope for a promotion or pay raise, show how improvement in certain areas can bolster their case.
4. **Offer Smaller Steps**: If they have trouble accepting big changes, break the improvements into smaller, less intimidating actions.
5. **Hold Them Accountable**: If they continue ignoring feedback and it harms the team, formal performance management steps might be necessary.

Over time, some employees learn to see constructive feedback as helpful rather than threatening.

11.15 Cultural Sensitivities in Feedback

In a multicultural setting, methods of giving feedback can clash with different cultural norms. Some cultures value directness, while others prefer subtlety. Some employees might interpret certain wording as harsh. To handle this:

- **Learn Basic Norms**: If you have a multinational team, do some research about their communication preferences.
- **Use Neutral Language**: Phrases that are too blunt can shut down conversation. Soften them slightly if your team is more sensitive.

- **Ask for Clarification**: If you sense confusion or fear, gently prompt the employee to share what they understood from your words.
- **Keep an Adaptable Style**: Remain open-minded about feedback methods. What works well for one group might need adjustments for another.

Balancing directness with respect is vital for leaders in global or diverse workplaces.

11.16 Encouraging Peer Feedback

Top-performing teams often share observations and tips among themselves, not only from boss to employee. Benefits include:

1. **Faster Corrections**: Colleagues can spot mistakes immediately and suggest solutions.
2. **Shared Learning**: Team members learn from each other's strengths.
3. **Less Hierarchical Pressure**: Employees might feel more relaxed learning from peers rather than from a manager.
4. **Team Cohesion**: Sharing feedback fosters mutual respect and better communication.

To foster peer feedback, define guidelines—remind everyone to keep it constructive, polite, and solution-oriented.

11.17 Recognizing Improvements

Although we must avoid certain words, you can still show genuine appreciation for growth:

- **Public Mentions**: During a team meeting, applaud an employee's effort to master a new skill or fix a recurring problem.
- **Written Notes**: A short message praising a recent achievement can mean a lot, especially if it is sincere and specific.
- **One-on-One Thanks**: Simply telling someone face-to-face that you noticed their progress can boost morale significantly.

- **Small Rewards**: If allowed by company policy, a small token or a bit of extra autonomy on a project can reinforce good work.

Such acknowledgment strengthens positive behaviors and reassures employees that their extra effort does not go unnoticed.

11.18 Regularly Reviewing the Measurement and Feedback System

No performance measurement or feedback mechanism is perfect forever. Factors that call for periodic reviews include:

1. **Changes in Company Strategy**: If the firm shifts focus from product features to service quality, you must adjust indicators accordingly.
2. **Team Growth**: As more members join, your old feedback routines might become cumbersome.
3. **Technological Advances**: New software or automated dashboards may streamline how you capture and present data.
4. **Employee Suggestions**: Staff might point out flaws in the current system or propose simpler ways to track results.

Staying flexible keeps the process relevant and prevents stagnation.

11.19 Long-Term Benefits of Good Measurement and Feedback

Well-executed measurement and feedback routines can:

- **Nurture a Growth Mindset**: Employees see that steady progress is valued.
- **Strengthen Trust**: Transparent metrics and fair feedback build credibility.
- **Boost Team Spirit**: Everyone knows what is expected, reducing finger-pointing or anxiety over hidden standards.
- **Improve Retention**: Workers are more likely to stay where they feel guided, appreciated, and challenged.

- **Drive Innovation**: By highlighting what works and what does not, teams can refine processes, adopt new ideas, and reach higher levels of performance.

Over time, this environment sets the stage for a resilient, forward-thinking workforce.

11.20 Conclusion of Chapter 11

Measuring performance and providing feedback are core leadership responsibilities. By selecting relevant indicators, avoiding common traps, and delivering feedback skillfully, you shape an atmosphere of continuous learning. A balanced approach—one that praises good work, addresses issues early, and encourages open dialogue—helps each person grow and keeps projects on course.

In the next chapter, we will examine a related topic: encouraging personal accountability. While measurements and feedback highlight what needs to be done, accountability ensures that individuals take ownership of their roles and outcomes. When combined, these practices equip a team to remain focused, motivated, and ready to tackle challenges without passing blame or shirking duties.

Chapter 12: Encouraging Personal Accountability

Accountability forms the backbone of a reliable, high-functioning team. Without it, projects can slip through the cracks, deadlines can be missed, and a culture of finger-pointing can emerge. By contrast, when employees take responsibility for their tasks, outcomes, and learning, they become more autonomous and driven. This chapter explores how you, as a boss, can create an environment that fosters personal accountability, outlining key strategies and avoiding the common pitfalls that undermine responsibility.

12.1 Defining Personal Accountability

Personal accountability means an individual accepts responsibility for their actions, decisions, and outcomes. Rather than blaming external factors or passing problems to someone else, accountable employees own up to mistakes, propose solutions, and learn from setbacks. Core traits of accountable people include:

1. **Dependability**: They complete tasks on time and to the expected standard.
2. **Honesty**: When issues occur, they acknowledge them rather than concealing or denying.
3. **Self-Motivation**: They take the initiative to solve problems, even when not directly ordered to do so.
4. **Continuous Learning**: They see errors as opportunities to refine their approach.

Leaders who reinforce these qualities see improved team performance and morale.

12.2 Why Accountability Matters

1. **Efficiency**: A workplace where everyone knows their responsibilities and follows through experiences fewer delays.
2. **Reduced Micromanagement**: When employees own their roles, bosses can focus on strategic leadership rather than constantly checking up.
3. **Better Team Relationships**: If each member pulls their weight, trust grows among colleagues.
4. **Faster Problem-Solving**: Accountable workers do not wait around for a manager to fix everything. They step up to find quick resolutions.
5. **Professional Growth**: Taking ownership encourages employees to learn more about their field, potentially preparing them for higher roles.

Without accountability, blame-shifting and repeated mistakes become the norm, undermining team spirit and overall results.

12.3 Common Barriers to Accountability

Even well-intentioned staff can struggle to stay accountable. Some reasons:

1. **Unclear Goals**: If employees are not sure what is expected, they cannot be fully responsible for results.
2. **Lack of Autonomy**: Overbearing bosses or rigid processes leave little room for personal decision-making, which weakens ownership.
3. **Fear of Punishment**: A harsh environment might lead people to hide mistakes rather than admit them.
4. **Poor Communication**: If tasks are assigned in vague ways or feedback is inconsistent, employees may not realize their specific role.
5. **Weak Leadership Example**: If managers pass blame or shirk duties, employees notice and mirror that behavior.

Addressing these barriers is an important first step in building accountability.

12.4 Setting Clear Expectations

One of the best ways to encourage accountability is to define what success looks like. Consider:

- **SMART Goals**: Targets that are Specific, Measurable, Achievable, Relevant, and Time-bound.
- **Detailed Role Descriptions**: Each position should have a clear overview of core duties and how they tie into the bigger objectives.
- **Key Milestones**: If a project lasts months, define checkpoints where employees must show progress.
- **Open Dialogue**: Check that employees fully understand their tasks. Sometimes, they nod in agreement but remain uncertain.

Clarity removes excuses for missed deadlines or subpar results.

12.5 Empowering Employees with Autonomy

Responsibility can only flourish if people have enough freedom to make choices:

1. **Delegation of Authority**: Beyond assigning tasks, let employees decide how they accomplish them (within sensible limits).
2. **Decision Bounds**: Define which decisions are theirs to make. For instance, they can adjust project details under a certain budget level or time threshold.
3. **Encourage Initiative**: Praise or thank team members who spot issues and fix them without waiting for orders.
4. **Provide Resources**: If they lack necessary tools or training, responsibility becomes an empty phrase.

When individuals feel ownership of both the process and outcome, their sense of responsibility rises naturally.

12.6 Encouraging a Problem-Solving Mindset

A crucial aspect of accountability is employees willingly tackling obstacles:

- **Ask for Solutions, Not Excuses**: When someone reports a problem, encourage them to suggest at least one way to handle it.
- **Teach Root Cause Analysis**: Instead of quick fixes, help employees identify why an issue keeps repeating. This fosters deeper understanding and permanent solutions.

- **Promote Cross-Functional Support**: If a challenge spans multiple teams, reward those who collaborate to find an effective fix.
- **Model Curiosity**: When you, as the boss, show curiosity rather than anger at unexpected setbacks, employees learn to do the same.

This mindset shift prevents the blame game, turning mistakes into learning opportunities.

12.7 Using Accountability Agreements

An accountability agreement is a simple but powerful tool. It involves:

1. **Written Statements**: The employee outlines the task, expected result, deadline, and resources needed.
2. **Shared Commitments**: Both you and the employee sign or at least acknowledge the agreement.
3. **Defined Checkpoints**: Note when you will meet to review progress or adjust the plan if something changes.
4. **Consequences**: Clarify what happens if the goal is not met, such as extra training, resource reallocation, or a review of responsibilities.

While not always mandatory, such agreements bring clarity and a sense of personal contract that can raise motivation.

12.8 Handling Mistakes to Build Accountability

When employees err, how a boss reacts sets the tone for future behavior:

1. **Respond Calmly**: Overreacting will only push employees to cover up mistakes next time.
2. **Explore Causes**: Was there a misunderstanding of instructions? A resource gap? A training need?
3. **Help Create an Improvement Plan**: Decide on actions or skill-building to prevent repeating the same mistake.
4. **Acknowledge Ownership**: If an employee openly admits their fault, appreciate their honesty. That encourages a culture of responsibility.

By viewing errors as chances to learn, you reinforce accountability rather than stifle it.

12.9 Rewarding Accountable Behavior

Although we cannot use certain words, you can still notice and commend employees who show initiative, reliability, or honesty:

- **Personal Thanks**: A sincere one-on-one moment means a lot.
- **Team Recognition**: Briefly highlight a person's responsible behavior in a group meeting.
- **Extra Opportunities**: Grant them leadership of a project or provide advanced training.
- **Praise Emails**: Send a short message to the person and copy the team or higher-ups, stating the positive impact of their efforts.

Positive reinforcement encourages others to follow suit, boosting the entire team's sense of responsibility.

12.10 Dealing with Chronic Lack of Accountability

Some employees repeatedly fail to own their tasks. If you have tried basic fixes, consider more formal steps:

1. **Private Discussion**: Outline the repeated issues. Ask them to share why they believe this keeps happening.
2. **Set Clear Consequences**: If deadlines are missed again, detail what the outcome will be—perhaps a performance improvement plan or a reassignment.
3. **Provide Support**: Offer resources if they claim confusion or lack of skills. However, track whether they use the offered help.
4. **Know When to Escalate**: If all attempts fail and their lack of responsibility harms the team, a formal warning or even dismissal might be necessary.

Consistently ignoring these problems erodes morale and makes other employees question leadership fairness.

12.11 Linking Accountability to Team Culture

Accountability thrives in an environment where people feel safe admitting weaknesses and are confident that colleagues have their backs. To foster this:

1. **Emphasize Group Goals**: Remind people that success depends on each member doing their part.
2. **Encourage Peer Support**: Let employees help each other meet deadlines or refine solutions. This builds shared responsibility.
3. **Stay Transparent**: If upper management changes strategy or sets new targets, share information promptly so everyone knows the new direction.
4. **Lead by Example**: If you, as the boss, make a mistake, admit it. Show how you plan to fix it. This honesty reduces stigma around error admission.

By weaving accountability into the team's daily habits, you create a stable atmosphere of mutual trust.

12.12 Handling Accountability in Remote or Hybrid Teams

Distance can increase the risk of blurred responsibilities. Steps to ensure accountability in virtual settings:

1. **Daily or Weekly Check-Ins**: Short video calls or messages where each member states goals, progress, and any barriers.
2. **Clear Task Assignments**: Use project management platforms (Trello, Asana, etc.) with visible deadlines and owners.
3. **Encourage Visibility**: Ask members to update statuses on shared tools, so everyone sees what stage each project is in.
4. **Frequent Feedback**: Remote workers can feel isolated. Providing more regular feedback prevents them from drifting off track.

A structured process helps remote teams maintain a sense of responsibility despite physical distance.

12.13 Empowering Middle Managers to Drive Accountability

Not all accountability leadership comes directly from the top boss. Mid-level managers or team leads play an equally important role:

- **Training Them**: Show them how to encourage accountability, give feedback, and resolve conflicts.
- **Delegating Control**: Allow them to set and track performance indicators for their sub-teams.
- **Praise Their Achievements**: If they successfully improve accountability in their group, acknowledge that.
- **Monitor Consistency**: Ensure each manager applies accountability principles fairly, avoiding favoritism or extremes.

When mid-level leaders also promote accountability, it spreads throughout the organization more naturally.

12.14 Creating a No-Blame Review Process

Projects sometimes fail or miss their targets. When that happens, a "no-blame" post-project review helps the team learn:

1. **Focus on Facts**: Gather data about timelines, costs, and outcomes to see what caused shortfalls.
2. **Highlight Good Practices**: Recognize elements that worked and consider how to extend them.
3. **Identify Gaps**: Did the team lack certain skills or were there communication breakdowns?
4. **Assign Ownership of Fixes**: For each discovered problem, decide who will work on improving it next time.
5. **Avoid Scapegoating**: The purpose is to find solutions, not to punish individuals—unless unethical behavior occurred.

This approach encourages accountability by treating mistakes as shared learning points rather than triggers for blame.

12.15 Strengthening Accountability Through Peer Partnerships

Sometimes pairing employees as "accountability buddies" can reinforce responsible behavior:

- **Regular Check-Ins**: Buddies meet weekly or biweekly to discuss goals and progress.
- **Shared Reminders**: Each one can prompt the other to follow through on tasks.
- **Moral Support**: If one faces a setback, the partner can offer tips or encouragement.
- **Constructive Criticism**: Buddies can point out when the other is slipping without it feeling like a formal reprimand.

This informal method can be highly effective, provided both parties approach it seriously.

12.16 Communication Techniques to Boost Ownership

How you assign tasks or discuss them influences accountability:

1. **Use Direct Language**: Instead of "It would be nice if someone could look at this," say "Alex, please analyze the report by Friday and send me your findings."
2. **Confirm Understanding**: Ask the person to restate the task to ensure clarity.
3. **Set Realistic Deadlines**: Overly tight deadlines might cause rushed work or missed dates, eroding trust in the process.
4. **Ask for Commitment**: "Can you commit to finishing this by Thursday?" fosters a conscious agreement.

Clear, confident communication signals that you expect them to own the task and deliver results.

12.17 Combining Accountability with Team Flexibility

Accountability does not mean rigid control. In fact, a flexible environment can strengthen responsibility if managed correctly:

- **Adaptable Hours**: Some employees might excel working different schedules, as long as they meet targets.
- **Project-Based Goals**: Let staff choose how to reach milestones, as long as they uphold quality standards.
- **Cross-Training**: Encourage people to learn tasks outside their usual scope, so they can cover for each other in busy times.
- **Trust Building**: Show that you trust employees' judgment in small matters, and they will likely be more open about any obstacles they face.

Striking the balance between freedom and accountability can lead to a more creative, committed workforce.

12.18 Linking Accountability to Performance Reviews

Accountability should be a criterion in performance evaluations, not just output or skill alone:

1. **Track Follow-Through**: Did the employee keep their commitments and meet deadlines?
2. **Evaluate Proactivity**: Assess whether they often tackle issues independently or wait to be told.
3. **Look for Collaborative Accountability**: Do they help colleagues when a shared goal is at risk, or do they ignore the problem?
4. **Reward Responsible Conduct**: Recognizing accountability in official reviews shows you value more than just raw results.

This encourages employees to see accountability as a formal expectation, not an optional trait.

12.19 Overcoming Setbacks: Accountability During Crises

When a crisis hits—like a major system failure or a sudden market change—accountability may slip under stress. To maintain it:

- **Communicate Often**: Give clear updates on the crisis and what steps are being taken.
- **Outline Emergency Roles**: If normal structures are disrupted, clarify who decides on quick fixes.
- **Stay Calm Under Pressure**: If you panic, employees might scatter or hide mistakes.
- **Debrief Afterward**: Once the crisis is handled, revisit what worked and what did not, ensuring accountability lessons are learned.

Even in emergencies, accountability helps teams move faster and with less confusion.

12.20 Conclusion of Chapter 12

Encouraging personal accountability is essential for a healthy, productive workplace. By setting clear goals, granting the right level of autonomy, and reacting to mistakes with a solution-focused mindset, a boss can inspire employees to own their duties fully. Accountability also links closely with other leadership practices—like performance measurement, effective feedback, and open communication. When individuals take responsibility for outcomes, the team can adapt better, solve problems quicker, and trust one another more deeply.

Next, we will look at how to grow long-term business relationships inside and outside the organization. While personal accountability provides a strong internal framework, external alliances and strategic partnerships can also shape a leader's success. Building and maintaining such relationships requires many of the same qualities: clarity, trustworthiness, and respect for shared objectives. By combining accountability with strong relationship-building skills, a boss can drive sustainable growth and resilience in any competitive environment.

Chapter 13: Growing Long-Term Business Relationships

A strong boss does not just manage tasks within the organization; they also form valuable partnerships and connections with people and entities outside the company. These include clients, suppliers, mentors, and community figures. Building and sustaining these external relationships can provide consistent revenue, reliable collaboration, and positive word-of-mouth, all of which elevate the company's standing in its field. This chapter will explore how to develop, strengthen, and maintain these ties over time, showing why stable external alliances are as important as internal management practices.

13.1 Why Long-Term Relationships Matter

1. **Predictable Income and Opportunities**: Loyal clients or partners who trust your brand are more likely to stay with you, providing steady work or sales.
2. **Better Negotiating Power**: When you have an ongoing partnership, you can often discuss contract terms more flexibly, leading to cost savings or shared benefits.
3. **Shared Knowledge**: Long-term business allies sometimes share trade secrets or best practices, helping both sides progress more quickly.
4. **Crisis Support**: During tough times, a trustworthy partner can provide essential resources or advice that can help your company stay afloat.
5. **Reputation Building**: Being known for good relationships boosts your profile, attracting more potential collaborators and clients.

Clearly, strong external ties can help future-proof the business in unpredictable markets.

13.2 Identifying Key Stakeholders

The first step is figuring out which external entities have the greatest effect on your success. These may include:

1. **Top Clients/Customers**: Those who generate the most income or serve as reference points for your products or services.
2. **Suppliers and Vendors**: Reliable suppliers ensure smooth operations, from raw materials to tech support.
3. **Industry Influencers**: These could be recognized experts, notable bloggers, or media outlets that shape opinions in your sector.
4. **Local Community Leaders**: In many markets, support from local officials or neighborhood groups helps expand brand awareness.
5. **Professional Organizations**: Membership-based groups or associations can bring opportunities for networking, skills development, and collaboration.

By pinpointing these groups, you can direct your energy toward people whose connections will help the firm long term.

13.3 Foundations of Trust and Respect

No strong partnership can exist without trust. Whether you are dealing with a customer or a partner company, you must:

- **Keep Promises**: Deliver on what you promise—whether it is the timeline, quality, or scope of a project.
- **Communicate Honestly**: If challenges occur, share them early. Surprises destroy confidence.
- **Offer Fair Value**: Make sure that pricing, delivery terms, or mutual responsibilities are set at a level that benefits all sides reasonably.
- **Show Respect for Their Needs**: Partners want to feel seen and heard. Ask about their pain points and keep them in mind when proposing solutions.
- **Own Mistakes Quickly**: If your side slips up, admit it. Suggest a plan to correct the error and prevent recurrences.

These standards of trust apply in nearly every culture or sector. Consistent demonstration of reliability gradually cements your position as a preferred ally.

13.4 Building Rapport with Clients

Clients often form the backbone of your revenue stream, so investing in these relationships pays off:

1. **Regular Check-Ins**: Schedule calls or visits to update clients on progress, gather feedback, and show you care.
2. **Deep Understanding**: Learn about their business, industry, and unique challenges. The more you know, the more tailored your solutions become.
3. **Customize Solutions**: Instead of a one-size-fits-all approach, adapt your products or services to suit client-specific problems. This personal touch builds loyalty.
4. **Transparent Pricing and Contracts**: Ambiguous fee structures can erode trust. If extra costs might arise, warn the client in advance and explain why.
5. **Proactive Service**: Offer advice or improvements they might not have asked for, especially if it solves an issue they did not realize they had.

When you show genuine interest in client success, they are more likely to stay with you long term.

13.5 Strengthening Supplier and Vendor Ties

Suppliers provide the raw materials or services that keep your business running smoothly. Forming stable relationships with them can:

- **Ensure Consistent Quality**: A supplier who values your relationship will be less likely to ship flawed goods.
- **Secure Better Terms**: Long-standing clients often earn loyalty discounts or priority deliveries in peak season.
- **Co-Develop Solutions**: If you need a specialized part or service, a supplier who knows your needs might help in creating a custom solution.
- **Receive Early Warnings**: If raw material costs are likely to rise or a shipment is delayed, loyal suppliers will inform you quickly so you can plan.

Respect in these ties goes both ways. Pay invoices on time, honor contracts, and avoid last-minute order changes unless absolutely necessary.

13.6 Effective Networking Strategies

Networking is not just about handing out business cards. It involves building meaningful connections that could blossom into partnerships or opportunities:

1. **Choose Events Wisely**: Attend conferences, meetups, or seminars relevant to your field. Large gatherings may not always yield the best contacts, so pick selectively.
2. **Set Clear Goals**: Before going to an event, decide what kind of people or companies you hope to meet. This gives you a focus while mingling.
3. **Listen More Than You Talk**: People appreciate someone who is genuinely curious about their work. Ask questions and reflect back what you hear, showing you are engaged.
4. **Follow Up Promptly**: After meeting someone, send a short note or message thanking them for their time. Suggest a next step if there is mutual interest.
5. **Offer Help**: Networking is not just about getting something; it is also about providing value. If you can introduce your new contact to someone helpful or share a piece of knowledge, do it.

A boss who consistently networks with authenticity soon finds that people reciprocate, opening doors to new endeavors.

13.7 Using Social Platforms and Online Presence

In many industries, online presence has become a key factor in maintaining relationships:

- **LinkedIn and Professional Platforms**: Regularly post updates, industry insights, or achievements to keep your network informed.
- **Company Website**: Ensure it presents your services, case studies, and contact details in a straightforward way. Make it easy for potential partners to see how you can help them.
- **Webinars and Podcasts**: Hosting or participating in discussions about industry topics can position you and your company as thought leaders, drawing possible collaborators.

- **Online Groups and Forums**: Platforms exist for virtually every niche. Engaging in relevant groups helps you stay up-to-date and connect with new prospects.

Proper use of these digital channels keeps your relationships fresh, even if face-to-face meetings happen infrequently.

13.8 Balancing Professional and Personal Elements

Relationships in business often mix professional aims with personal rapport. While there is a line not to cross, showing a bit of humanity can be valuable:

1. **Light Personal Topics**: Asking about a partner's hobbies, family events, or weekend plans fosters warmth without invading privacy.
2. **Friendly Gestures**: A short note on someone's birthday or a small congratulatory message for a major milestone is enough to stand out.
3. **Holiday Acknowledgments**: Simple greetings during festive times (if culturally appropriate) remind them you value the relationship.
4. **Avoid Overstepping**: Stay respectful if they seem guarded. Some people like to keep matters strictly professional.

Striking this balance makes you more than just a provider of services—people enjoy working with those they find approachable and sincere.

13.9 Addressing Conflicts in Business Relationships

No matter how carefully you manage ties, disagreements can arise. Resolving them quickly and respectfully can strengthen rather than weaken a bond:

- **Stay Calm**: Emotions can flare when money or reputations are at risk, but a level head helps find solutions.
- **Gather Facts**: Collect relevant data on the issue—deliveries, emails, contracts, or any other records.
- **Seek a Win-Win**: Aim for a resolution that respects both parties' needs. If someone clearly made an error, they should be prepared to correct it.

- **Apologize When Necessary**: A genuine apology for a mistake goes a long way toward repairing trust. Follow it with corrective actions.
- **Involve Third Parties if Needed**: Sometimes a neutral mediator or industry association helps if the conflict becomes complicated.

Handled well, conflict can actually deepen the mutual respect as both sides see that the relationship can survive difficult moments.

13.10 Collaborations and Co-Branding

Partnerships can range from casual supplier-buyer setups to deeper collaborations that boost visibility for both sides:

1. **Joint Ventures**: Two organizations might form a temporary or permanent alliance to tackle a new market or develop a fresh product.
2. **Co-Marketing**: Partnering on a marketing campaign, such as a webinar or special event, widens reach for both parties.
3. **Cross-Promotions**: Each business features the other's service. For example, a web design firm might recommend a digital marketing agency in return for the same.
4. **Resource Sharing**: If you have a large mailing list and your partner has valuable content, you both benefit by introducing each other's assets to new audiences.

Such collaboration can amplify brand awareness and bring in extra revenue streams.

13.11 The Role of Industry Events and Conferences

Industry gatherings, from small workshops to large expos, remain a prime environment for nurturing existing ties:

- **Invitations to Key Contacts**: Let your best clients or partners know you will be at a particular event. Offer to meet for coffee or attend a session together.

- **Speaking Engagements**: If possible, speak on a panel or give a talk. This positions you as a subject expert, helping reinforce credibility.
- **Sponsor Opportunities**: Businesses sometimes sponsor parts of the event—like a lounge or workshop—gaining brand visibility and goodwill.
- **Team Representation**: Bring relevant staff who can connect directly with prospective partners. Ensure they understand your goals, so they gather leads effectively.

A face-to-face meeting often cements rapport in a way digital methods cannot achieve alone.

13.12 Corporate Social Responsibility (CSR) and Community Ties

Helping the community can be more than just philanthropy—it can form a constructive relationship with local groups:

1. **Participating in Local Programs**: Whether it is volunteering time or donating resources, being active in the community builds goodwill.
2. **Sponsoring Events**: Supporting cultural, educational, or health events in the region can boost name recognition and respect.
3. **Environmental Initiatives**: Some partners value eco-friendly practices. Show them you reduce waste, save energy, or promote green policies.
4. **Open Dialogue**: Listen to community leaders' suggestions on how your business can assist. This cultivates trust and a sense of shared purpose.

By balancing community involvement with business aims, you anchor your firm as a supportive neighbor rather than just a profit-seeking entity.

13.13 Sustaining Relationships Over Time

Forming relationships is one thing; maintaining them is another. Strategies include:

1. **Routine Communication**: Don't wait until you need something to reach out. Share updates or say hello occasionally.

2. **Anniversary Recognition**: Mark the date when a client first signed on or a partnership began. A quick, friendly note keeps the relationship fresh.
3. **Adapting to Their Growth**: As your partner's needs evolve, update your service offerings or skill sets so you remain relevant.
4. **Client/Partner Satisfaction Surveys**: Brief questionnaires help you spot potential dissatisfaction or new opportunities to serve them better.

Consistent effort ensures you do not drift apart or get blindsided by changing demands.

13.14 Technology Tools for Relationship Management

Several software options exist to simplify tracking and interaction with your network:

- **CRM Systems**: Customer Relationship Management platforms (Salesforce, HubSpot, etc.) store contact details, notes, and reminders for follow-up.
- **Email Marketing Tools**: Automated newsletters or drip campaigns keep contacts engaged without spamming them.
- **Project Collaboration Apps**: Tools like Slack or Microsoft Teams can help you communicate with partners in real-time, sharing files and updates quickly.
- **Analytics Dashboards**: Keep an eye on how your marketing efforts—like campaigns or webinars—affect leads or client retention.

These tools reduce the chance that important connections slip through the cracks.

13.15 Handling Growth and Scaling Up

As your business grows, so do your relationship demands. You may need more staff to handle increasing client volumes or to manage multiple supplier deals. Points to consider:

1. **Hiring Relationship Managers**: If you have many high-value clients or complex partnerships, dedicated staff can maintain personalized attention.
2. **Establishing Clear Procedures**: Scripts, guidelines, or brand voice documents help all team members interact with external parties consistently.
3. **Training**: Teach new and existing employees how to talk with clients politely, track interactions, and handle problems.
4. **Prioritizing Key Accounts**: When resources are limited, focus on the highest-potential or most profitable relationships first.

Scaling in a thoughtful way ensures that quality of connection does not suffer as quantity grows.

13.16 Merging Internal and External Perspectives

Building internal alignment helps ensure everyone in the company understands the importance of external relationships:

- **Briefing Your Team**: Share details about vital client accounts, key suppliers, or strategic partners.
- **Cross-Functional Collaboration**: Encourage multiple departments (sales, operations, finance) to cooperate in serving a major partner.
- **Feedback Loops**: Gather internal feedback on whether certain clients are causing undue strain or if a supplier's demands are out of line.
- **Encourage Empathy**: Remind employees that external partners often face pressures of their own, so quick blame or frustration is not productive.

When the whole organization values external ties, relationships have a stronger foundation.

13.17 Recognizing Shifting Markets or Technology Changes

Industries and markets never stay static. A good boss monitors trends that might affect existing alliances:

1. **Watch Competitors**: If a competitor offers more advanced features or lower prices, your partner might be tempted to switch. Adapt quickly.
2. **Stay Technologically Current**: Lagging behind in digital tools or platforms can make you seem old-fashioned to modern clients.
3. **Forecast Economic Shifts**: If certain materials or labor costs rise globally, discuss strategies with your suppliers to handle the impact.
4. **Refine Contracts**: Remain open to revising terms or service levels as the environment changes.

Being flexible and forward-thinking can preserve loyalty even in times of big market swings.

13.18 Overcoming Relationship Setbacks

Sometimes a partnership hits a rough patch—a missed delivery, a communication mix-up, or an argument over fees. To recover:

- **Address the Issue Directly**: Do not let misunderstandings fester. Arrange a call or meeting to clear the air.
- **Adjust Terms if Needed**: Offer a discount, a contract extension, or added services if it helps repair trust.
- **Learn from Mistakes**: Put safeguards in place to prevent repeats, such as better deadlines or clearer scopes of work.
- **Reassure and Rebuild**: Send a follow-up note confirming your renewed commitment to making the relationship productive.

Rebuilding trust can strengthen the bond, showing that you stand by your partners in good times and bad.

13.19 The Value of Mentors and Advisors

While often overlooked, mentors and professional advisors are valuable external relationships:

1. **Industry Expertise**: Advisors with years of experience can warn you of pitfalls and offer tested insights.

2. **Networking Connections**: Mentors may introduce you to influential figures or potential investors.
3. **Moral Support**: Leadership can be isolating. Mentors provide a safe space to discuss uncertainties and gain fresh perspectives.
4. **Ongoing Learning**: They might suggest courses, books, or conferences to keep your skills relevant.

Cultivating a strong relationship with a mentor or advisory board can have a lasting influence on your success trajectory.

13.20 Conclusion of Chapter 13

Long-term business relationships are a cornerstone of sustainable success. By identifying key stakeholders, building trust and respect, resolving conflicts swiftly, and adapting to changing circumstances, a boss can shape a network that boosts profitability, resilience, and innovation. From clients and suppliers to mentors and community leaders, each connection carries its own potential for mutual growth. Nurturing these bonds requires consistency, empathy, and strategic thinking.

In the next chapter, we will discuss how to motivate teams through rewards and recognition—without using forbidden terms. Recognizing good performance and consistent effort not only fuels employee morale but also helps solidify the healthy environment you have worked to create. By linking recognition programs to accountability and relationship-building, you can propel the team to aim higher and stay dedicated to the organization's goals.

Chapter 14: Motivating Through Rewards and Recognition

A boss who wants consistent high-level performance must acknowledge the employees' need for appreciation. Workers who feel invisible or underappreciated eventually lose motivation and might start looking for other opportunities. On the other hand, those who receive sincere, well-structured rewards often perform even better, increasing productivity and strengthening loyalty. This chapter explores diverse ways to commend excellent work, from public praise to structured bonuses, all while avoiding certain terms that might seem overused or too flowery. Instead, we focus on genuine, practical steps that keep teams energized.

14.1 Why Recognition Matters

1. **Psychological Boost**: Being noticed for positive contributions triggers a sense of accomplishment, fueling morale and reducing burnout.
2. **Reinforcement of Desired Behaviors**: When you highlight the behaviors or outcomes you want, others see what to replicate.
3. **Stronger Retention**: Employees who feel valued are more likely to stay, lowering turnover costs.
4. **Culture Building**: Ongoing recognition shapes a supportive atmosphere where people lift each other up.
5. **Alignment with Goals**: By aligning rewards with company objectives, you guide everyone toward the same vision.

If your workplace never acknowledges achievements, staff may interpret that as indifference, killing motivation.

14.2 Moving Beyond the Generic "Good Job"

While praising someone is good, generic words do not show depth. More effective methods:

- **Be Specific**: State exactly what the employee did well. For example, "Your quick rework of the sales data helped us meet the client's deadline."
- **Mention Impact**: Tie the behavior to a result: "Because of your extra hours, we secured the contract. That means stable funding for the next quarter."
- **Personal Connection**: Use their name, reference personal growth or unique skills they displayed.
- **Acknowledge Challenges**: If they overcame a complex issue or worked under tough constraints, highlight that, too.

This approach shows employees you are paying attention, not just handing out blanket compliments.

14.3 Types of Rewards and Recognitions

1. **Verbal Praise**: Simple yet powerful. A short statement in a team meeting or a private chat can do wonders.
2. **Written Notes**: Handwritten letters or emails that detail the achievement can be kept as a reminder of success.
3. **Public Forums**: Mention stellar performance in a company newsletter or during a larger event to let everyone see the excellence.
4. **Material Tokens**: These might include gift cards, small bonuses, or items with the company logo. Although these can please employees, they should accompany genuine words of thanks.
5. **Opportunity-Based**: Extra training options, attendance at conferences, or leading a new project can be more valuable than cash alone.
6. **Peer Recognition Programs**: Systems where employees nominate each other for outstanding efforts help foster a team-focused environment.

Each method has its place. Vary them based on the level and nature of the accomplishment.

14.4 Aligning Rewards with Company Values

If your firm champions customer satisfaction, you might specifically reward employees who go the extra mile in client service. If innovation is central, highlight creative solutions that save money or boost revenue. This ensures employees realize that the skills and results you celebrate align with the broader mission, so recognition becomes both motivational and educational. They know, "If I prioritize these values, the company will acknowledge me."

14.5 Recognizing Team Efforts

Not all achievements result from one person's input. Often, a team's collective effort drives large wins. Ways to show team appreciation:

- **Group Applause**: During a department meeting, briefly summarize the project's success and mention the key contributors.
- **Shared Perks**: Provide a group lunch, a fun team-building day, or simple in-office goodies to mark the milestone.
- **Team Spotlight**: A short write-up on the company intranet or a bulletin board explaining how the team collaborated.
- **Special Projects**: Let the successful team handle a more interesting or high-profile assignment next, recognizing their proven synergy.

Team-based recognition underlines the idea that cooperation and unity are valued behaviors.

14.6 Balancing Individual and Group Recognition

While praising teams fosters unity, it is also important to note when individuals stand out:

1. **Avoid Overemphasis on One Person**: If a project was a group effort, focusing on just one star performer might demoralize others.
2. **Pinpoint Unique Contributions**: It's possible to say, "The entire team worked hard. Additionally, Alex's data analysis was crucial to making sure our approach was accurate."

3. **No Favorites**: Distribute individual praise fairly. If you repeatedly single out the same person, others might feel overlooked, unless that individual truly surpasses expectations every time.
4. **Let Peers Nominate**: Sometimes employees see contributions that a boss might miss. Give them a channel to highlight a coworker's outstanding help.

A balanced approach creates both collaborative spirit and fair acknowledgment for standout actions.

14.7 Timing: When to Recognize

Timeliness is critical. Delaying recognition for months waters down its impact:

- **Immediate**: Small wins, daily tasks done exceptionally well—give quick praise.
- **Short-Term**: For mid-level successes, a weekly or monthly highlight is reasonable.
- **Major Milestones**: Big projects might merit a more formal recognition after completion, such as at a quarterly meeting.
- **Annual**: Certain achievements, such as record-breaking sales or longstanding excellence, might fit a yearly award ceremony or performance review mention.

Avoid letting good work go unnoticed until the next official evaluation; real-time boosts are more powerful.

14.8 Avoiding the Trap of Empty Rewards

Some bosses dish out frequent "awards" that employees see as hollow. Pitfalls include:

1. **Constant Praise Without Substance**: If everything is "excellent," the words lose meaning.
2. **Overuse of Trivial Items**: Cheap tokens handed out for minimal tasks can feel patronizing.

3. **Ignoring Real Problems**: If staff are overworked or poorly paid, small "prizes" may seem like a poor substitute for actual support.
4. **Bias or Favoritism**: If an award system is unclear or obviously skewed, employees become cynical.
5. **Rewarding for Basic Duties**: Congratulating employees just for meeting normal expectations might lower the bar overall.

Authenticity and fairness are vital to ensure workers trust the recognition process.

14.9 Linking Rewards to Performance Metrics

A fair system often uses measurable outcomes. Possible metrics:

- **Sales Growth**: Extra reward if someone exceeds a set sales target by a certain percentage.
- **Quality Benchmarks**: Recognition for those who reduce error rates or customer complaints.
- **Process Improvements**: Highlight cost savings or productivity boosts that an employee's idea enabled.
- **Teamwork Indicators**: If peers consistently mention someone's supportive attitude, it could merit a reward.
- **Customer Endorsements**: Positive feedback from clients might trigger a note of thanks or a public mention.

Basing rewards on transparent numbers or documented achievements reduces accusations of bias.

14.10 Low-Cost and Creative Incentives

Not every company has a large budget for bonuses. Even small gestures can have a big impact when done thoughtfully:

1. **Prime Parking Spots**: Allow a top performer to park closer to the building for a week.

2. **Flexible Scheduling**: Offer the chance to start late or leave early on a chosen day.
3. **Office Perks**: A favorite snack on their desk or access to a quiet lounge for a week.
4. **Learning Credits**: A coupon for an online course or workshop in their area of interest.
5. **Supportive Mentoring**: Pair the recognized employee with a senior mentor for extra career guidance.

By applying a bit of imagination, you can inspire morale without draining resources.

14.11 Personalized Approaches to Recognition

Not all employees are the same. Some prefer public applause, while others cringe at the spotlight:

- **Ask for Preferences**: If someone is shy, a one-on-one note or private chat might mean more.
- **Consider Generational Differences**: Younger staff might value career development opportunities, while more seasoned workers may like flexible time off or expanded responsibility.
- **Balance Big and Small**: Introverts may appreciate a subtle mention, while extroverts might enjoy receiving an award at a group gathering.
- **Cultural Sensitivities**: In certain cultures, public displays of praise can feel awkward or boastful, so adapt accordingly.

Tailoring your approach shows genuine respect for individual differences.

14.12 Encouraging Peer-to-Peer Recognition

People often value kind words from colleagues more than official applause from the top. Possible setups include:

1. **Recognition Boards**: A physical or online board where employees write notes praising each other's work.

2. **Nomination Systems**: A monthly process where staff members nominate a peer who went beyond basic duties.
3. **Weekly Shout-Outs**: During team meetings, allow a few moments for anyone to highlight a colleague's assistance.
4. **Team Rewards**: If employees collectively pick a coworker who consistently helps them, let that winner choose a perk (like a small item or a beneficial schedule).

Peer-driven recognition fosters camaraderie and reminds everyone that success is a group effort.

14.13 Leadership Visibility and Recognition

A boss's presence at recognition moments can amplify impact:

- **Attend Team Celebrations**: If a department hits a milestone, drop by personally and share congratulatory words.
- **Co-Sign Letters or Emails**: When awarding a certificate or sending a note, add your personal signature or message.
- **Meet in Person**: A one-on-one meeting where you express gratitude can stay in an employee's memory for a long time.
- **Link to Career Growth**: Mention how the recognized trait could position them for a promotion or leadership role down the line.

Your time and attention is a priceless resource; using it to show appreciation signals that the person truly matters.

14.14 Recognizing Effort Versus Results

Some accomplishments are clear-cut (landing a major contract), but what about the times an employee pours heart into a project that ultimately stalls?

1. **Effort Matters**: If an employee displayed creativity or determination, show gratitude for that, even if results were outside their control.
2. **Focus on Learning**: Praise the lessons gleaned from setbacks. This builds a culture unafraid of experimentation.

3. **Be Honest**: If the final outcome fell short, do not pretend otherwise. Acknowledge the shortfall but highlight the positives.
4. **Encourage Improvement**: Offer ways to refine methods or gather feedback for next time.

Striking this balance prevents staff from feeling only final outcomes get noticed. It also inspires resilience and a mindset that values continuous growth.

14.15 Making Recognition Part of the Daily Culture

Recognition should not be rare or only top-down. Integrate it into everyday norms:

- **Regular Feedback Loops**: Encourage managers to praise helpful acts or good work as soon as they see it.
- **Begin Meetings with Positivity**: Start some meetings by letting anyone mention a recent act they found impressive.
- **Departmental Highlights**: In weekly or monthly reports, include a section for spotlighting notable achievements.
- **Micro-Moments**: Even a quick "thank you" as you pass someone's desk shows thoughtfulness.

Small, repeated gestures can outshine an occasional big ceremony in terms of daily motivation.

14.16 Handling Envy or Negative Reactions

Sometimes, employees who do not receive recognition might feel overlooked. They might question the fairness of the process. To address this:

1. **Be Transparent**: If there is a formal system, make sure everyone knows the criteria and can see why a certain person was rewarded.
2. **Encourage Open Dialogue**: Invite employees to discuss concerns if they believe recognition is imbalanced.
3. **Publicly Highlight Everyone Over Time**: Maybe you rotate recognition focuses or ensure that different projects have a chance to shine.

4. **Review Your Data**: If only a specific department or a handful of people keep getting praised, verify if that is indeed performance-based or if you are unconsciously overlooking others.

Openness reduces suspicion and helps maintain a supportive environment.

14.17 Using Technology for Recognition Programs

Online tools can streamline or enhance your approach:

- **Employee Platforms**: Some systems let coworkers give each other "badges" or points for various positive actions.
- **Automated Milestone Alerts**: Tech can remind you of work anniversaries, project completions, or personal achievements.
- **Tracking Achievements**: A database can log recognized feats, so employees can see a clear record of their growth over time.
- **Gamification Elements**: Points, leaderboards, or levels can work if used sparingly, but avoid turning everything into a shallow competition.

Technology must supplement genuine human feedback, not replace it.

14.18 Handling Bigger Rewards and Bonuses

Apart from daily acknowledgment, larger rewards might be relevant for major projects or record-breaking performances:

1. **Financial Bonuses**: Tied to specific metrics—like hitting sales targets or completing a major project under budget.
2. **Stock Options**: In some companies, key staff receive shares, giving them a stake in overall success.
3. **Paid Vacations**: An extra day or two off, or even a travel voucher, can be a nice perk.
4. **Career Advancement**: Promotion opportunities often serve as the most impactful form of recognition for ambitious employees.

Structure these bigger incentives carefully to avoid creating unintended competition or overshadowing small but meaningful progress.

14.19 Periodic Reviews and Adjustments

A recognition system must stay flexible:

- **Survey Employees**: Ask for feedback on which rewards resonate most. Some ideas may lose their charm over time.
- **Observe Patterns**: Is there a spike in morale or performance following certain programs? Which recognition methods fail to generate enthusiasm?
- **Rotate Rewards**: If your staff sees the same small gifts again and again, interest might dwindle. Mix in new ideas or perks.
- **Consider External Factors**: In economic downturns, employees might appreciate financial help more than symbolic tokens. Adjust accordingly.

Periodic checks ensure you keep the program fresh and aligned with shifting workforce needs.

14.20 Conclusion of Chapter 14

Recognition and rewards, when done thoughtfully, energize a team and amplify positive behaviors. It is not about fancy phrases or over-the-top ceremonies but about clear, consistent praise that shows employees they matter. By combining daily acknowledgments with occasional bigger perks, aligning honors with company values, and respecting individual preferences, you create a culture where people feel motivated to excel. Avoiding empty gestures or favoritism ensures trust remains strong, and employees believe the system is fair.

In the upcoming chapters, we will continue looking at advanced leadership insights, including how to handle stress and burnout, foster creativity, refine decision-making skills, and much more. All these aspects tie into being a well-rounded boss who not only pushes productivity but also supports the well-being and professional growth of the team. By weaving recognition into each part of your management style, you position yourself as a leader who genuinely appreciates people's efforts—and that is a major step toward ongoing success.

Chapter 15: Handling Stress and Burnout

The pace of modern business can be punishing. Rapid deadlines, complex tasks, and high expectations often push leaders and their staff to the limit. Even the most capable bosses can find themselves overwhelmed, risking both personal well-being and team productivity. Stress in small amounts can motivate people to perform at their peak, but when it becomes chronic, it leads to exhaustion, reduced output, and health problems. This chapter explores how to handle stress and prevent burnout—both for yourself and your team—by presenting practical approaches that go beyond obvious advice.

15.1 Understanding the Roots of Workplace Stress

1. **Excessive Workloads**: Tight deadlines, long hours, and a constant backlog of tasks can drain energy.
2. **Unclear Expectations**: If an employee (or even a manager) is unsure of their role or goals, anxiety rises.
3. **Poor Resource Allocation**: When staff lack the tools or training needed, stress escalates as they try to meet demands with inadequate support.
4. **Mismatch in Values**: If the company's values clash with personal beliefs—like ethical practices or work-life balance—stress levels increase.
5. **Constant Interruptions**: Frequent emails, calls, and messages disrupt flow, forcing people to multitask or shift focus too often.

Recognizing these factors helps you intervene early instead of waiting until morale drops or deadlines are missed.

15.2 The Physical and Mental Toll of Ongoing Stress

Unmanaged stress can damage both body and mind:

- **Health Issues**: Chronic stress can lead to headaches, stomach problems, and elevated blood pressure. Over time, this may contribute to more serious conditions like heart disease.
- **Reduced Mental Sharpness**: Prolonged anxiety undermines concentration, creativity, and decision-making.

- **Emotional Burnout**: Individuals may feel apathetic or disengaged, losing the drive that once fueled their productivity.
- **Sleep Disruption**: Stress often causes insomnia or poor-quality rest, leading to sluggish days.
- **Tense Relationships**: Irritability can surface, causing conflicts with colleagues, clients, or loved ones at home.

Leaders need to be aware not just of their own well-being but also watch for warning signs in team members. Early detection can prevent bigger crises.

15.3 Strategies for Personal Stress Management

A boss under constant stress cannot guide effectively. You must begin by taking care of your own mental health:

1. **Set Realistic Limits**: You cannot do everything at once. Learn to say "no" politely when a request is unmanageable or not aligned with priorities.
2. **Time Blocking**: Allocate segments of your schedule to work on specific tasks without interruption. This reduces the chaos of multitasking.
3. **Delegate Wisely**: Passing tasks to capable team members lightens your load and helps them grow. Micromanaging undoes these benefits, so let them handle the details.
4. **Short Breaks**: Step away for a few minutes to recharge. Even a short walk or a quick stretch can reset your mind.
5. **Lifestyle Habits**: Aim for balanced meals, physical movement, and consistent sleep. While this may sound obvious, many leaders overlook these basics when busy.

By first addressing your own stress, you set a healthy example for others.

15.4 Recognizing Burnout in Yourself and Others

Burnout goes beyond regular fatigue. It is a deeper sense of disconnection and weariness that does not improve with short breaks:

- **Emotional Exhaustion**: Feeling constantly drained, even when tasks are not excessive.

- **Detachment**: A cynical attitude toward work, coworkers, or the company.
- **Reduced Efficiency**: Projects take longer, errors increase, or deadlines are missed more often.
- **Low Enthusiasm**: Tasks that once inspired motivation feel pointless or burdensome.
- **Physical Signs**: Insomnia, frequent illnesses, lingering fatigue, and muscle tension.

As a boss, do not label someone as "lazy" if they show these symptoms. Instead, approach them with concern and explore whether changes in workload or environment could help.

15.5 Reducing Stress at the Organizational Level

While personal coping strategies matter, it is also vital to create a workplace that does not feed stress:

1. **Realistic Goals and Deadlines**: Confirm that timelines match the actual resources available. Overcommitment fosters panic rather than excellence.
2. **Clarify Roles**: Ensure everyone knows their responsibilities. Overlapping tasks or vague instructions cause confusion and tension.
3. **Prioritize Projects**: Not everything is equally urgent. Label tasks as critical, important, or flexible so the team knows where to focus.
4. **Open Communication**: Encourage employees to voice concerns if they see a bottleneck coming. Early warnings let you adjust before a crisis hits.
5. **Sensible Policies**: For instance, discourage sending emails at odd hours unless critical. This small change can reduce after-hours stress.

When people see you actively minimize structural stressors, they trust your leadership more and feel safer reporting issues.

15.6 Tactics to Support the Team's Well-Being

1. **Flexible Schedules**: Where possible, let employees adjust start times or work from home occasionally, aiding them in balancing personal and professional needs.

2. **Resource Provision**: Provide training, software, or additional staff if the workload grows. Lack of support fuels frustration.
3. **Encourage Breaks**: Some organizations adopt short "reset" periods or quiet zones where staff can step away from tasks.
4. **Create a Safe Space for Dialogue**: Hold regular check-ins, asking about workload balance. Make it normal to discuss stress without shame.
5. **Offer Guidance**: If a team member is struggling, suggest they consult a professional counselor or an employee assistance program if available.

These measures show that leadership values mental health. In turn, employees are likelier to stay motivated and loyal.

15.7 Role of Proper Task Delegation in Stress Control

A frequent cause of stress is an uneven workload. Delegation is not about offloading random tasks; it is about distributing responsibilities in a way that:

- **Matches Skills**: Assign tasks in line with each person's talents so they feel challenged but not overwhelmed.
- **Allows Growth**: Let rising talents handle slightly more complex duties under your guidance, strengthening their confidence.
- **Prevents Bottlenecks**: If too many key tasks rely on one overburdened team member, a single absence or burnout can stop progress.
- **Builds Trust**: Over time, employees see that the boss trusts them to manage important aspects of a project.

Good delegation not only eases your own load but also raises morale across the team.

15.8 Mindful Leadership Approaches

Leaders who practice mindfulness often cope better with stress. You do not have to commit to lengthy meditation sessions; small habits can help:

1. **Daily Pauses**: Spend a minute focusing on your breath before a major meeting or after reading a stressful email.

2. **Attentive Listening**: When someone speaks, truly focus on them. This reduces mental clutter and prevents misunderstandings.
3. **Self-Check**: Periodically ask yourself, "Am I tense? Is my mind racing?" If yes, take a brief moment to calm down.
4. **Model Emotional Balance**: If you remain calm under pressure, the team is more likely to follow suit, reducing overall stress.

Even short, mindful pauses can reset tension and keep you grounded during hectic days.

15.9 Setting Boundaries Between Work and Personal Life

Modern technology makes it easy to work anywhere, anytime. While flexible work can be helpful, it can also rob employees of rest:

- **Limit Off-Hours Work**: If urgent issues must be handled at night, rotate responsibilities so the same person is not always on call.
- **Encourage Vacations**: Make sure people use their allotted time off, and avoid contacting them with non-urgent matters during their break.
- **Lead by Example**: If you email staff late at night, they may feel pressured to reply immediately. Schedule messages to send in the morning or clearly state that a response can wait.
- **Respect Personal Boundaries**: Avoid expecting staff to attend weekend events or check messages during personal time, unless it is critical.

These practices protect everyone's personal time, lowering burnout risk.

15.10 Techniques for Handling Stressful Situations in Real-Time

Even with preventative measures, stressful moments arise—like a major client complaint or a sudden drop in sales:

1. **Pause and Breathe**: Take a few deep breaths to calm your racing mind before reacting.
2. **Gather Facts Quickly**: Confirm the details from reliable sources. Panicking over rumors can worsen confusion.

3. **Break Down Action Steps**: Identify immediate tasks and who will handle them, rather than letting chaos spread.
4. **Communicate Clearly**: Let the team know the plan, even if it is still forming. They want direction.
5. **Stay Composed Externally**: While you might feel stress inside, maintain a calm tone with employees, encouraging a measured response.

This disciplined approach can contain the situation and reassure everyone involved.

15.11 Preventing the Boss from Being the Only Problem Solver

When a boss tries to solve every issue alone, stress compounds:

- **Empower Others**: Encourage staff to try finding solutions on their own first, then bring options to you.
- **Create Experts**: Let certain employees become the "go-to" persons for specific problems. This relieves your plate and grows their expertise.
- **Reward Initiative**: Recognize those who step up to resolve conflicts or troubleshoot errors without waiting for orders.
- **Prepare a Succession Plan**: Train one or two people who can handle key leadership duties if you are absent or busy.

Spreading problem-solving responsibility prevents the boss from being overwhelmed and fosters a sense of ownership among the team.

15.12 Checking in with Remote or Hybrid Workers

In a partially remote world, it is harder to see signs of stress. Some employees might hide their struggles behind screens. To counter this:

1. **Frequent Video Calls**: Face-to-face contact, even via webcam, can show facial expressions that phone calls or chats might miss.
2. **Structured Updates**: Have them share a brief status update daily or weekly so you spot potential overload early.

3. **Encourage Online Social Spaces**: Virtual lounges or informal chat channels let remote staff share personal challenges or lighten the mood.
4. **Spot Subtle Cues**: Repeated late responses, missing deadlines, or frequent canceled calls may indicate stress. Ask them how they are coping.
5. **Flexible Arrangement**: A remote worker might need different schedule accommodations if they juggle household responsibilities.

Make sure distance does not breed isolation or make stress invisible.

15.13 Team Activities and Approaches to Ease Tension

Injecting light-hearted moments or supportive structures can reduce stress:

- **Group Learning**: Workshops on stress management, run by a professional, can equip everyone with coping tools.
- **Team Challenges**: Non-work challenges, like step-count competitions or shared reading goals, encourage healthy habits.
- **Acknowledgment Sessions**: Start a weekly meeting with staff mentioning good news or small achievements. This fosters a positive tone.
- **Buddy Systems**: Pair employees so they can check on each other, share tips, or swap tasks if one is overloaded.

These activities ensure the team bonds and that the mental load is not carried alone.

15.14 Avoiding Toxic Competition

In some workplaces, competitiveness goes too far. Employees fear losing out if they do not overwork themselves. To prevent this:

1. **Reward Collaboration**: Highlight teams or individuals who help others instead of focusing solely on solo achievements.
2. **Avoid "Hero" Culture**: Praising someone who works extreme hours without rest can normalize unhealthy behavior.
3. **Limit Leaderboard Pressures**: If sales or performance boards exist, keep them in perspective. Not everyone thrives under constant competition.

4. **Promote Shared Wins**: When a project succeeds, let everyone see how joint input was key. This combats any dog-eat-dog mentality.

A balanced approach encourages striving for excellence without sacrificing well-being.

15.15 Handling Special Situations: Personal Crises

Sometimes, stress comes from personal events—family illness, financial problems, or other crises that spill into work. A boss should:

- **Respect Privacy**: Let the employee decide how much detail to share. Do not pry.
- **Offer Adjustments**: If possible, offer flexible hours or a reduced workload temporarily to accommodate their needs.
- **Refer to Resources**: Point them to counseling programs or community help if your organization cannot fully address the matter.
- **Stay Compassionate**: Simple, understanding gestures can ease their stress immensely.
- **Monitor Impact on the Team**: While providing support, also ensure the rest of the team does not become overburdened or resentful.

A humane approach respects both the individual and business requirements.

15.16 The Boss's Role in Setting Healthy Norms

Leaders heavily influence the culture around stress:

1. **Walk the Talk**: If you preach work-life balance but send urgent messages at midnight, employees notice the contradiction.
2. **Be Transparent**: If you need time off or are reducing your schedule to handle personal stress, share that openly. This signals that it is acceptable to do so.
3. **Acknowledge Hard Work**: Let the team know you see their efforts, but also remind them to pace themselves.
4. **Encourage Self-Care**: Sometimes employees feel guilty taking breaks. Reinforce that short downtime can lead to better performance afterward.

When you set healthy norms, employees are more likely to respect those boundaries and remain stable under stress.

15.17 Building Resilience as a Team

Resilience is the capacity to handle challenges and rebound stronger:

- **Cross-Training**: When employees know more than one role, the team can absorb absences without major disruptions.
- **Regular Reflection**: After stressful projects, hold a quick review to see what worked and what needs improving next time.
- **Support Networks**: Encourage collaboration so no one is isolated with a heavy burden.
- **Growth Mindset**: Emphasize learning from setbacks rather than punishment. This helps people adapt to difficulties without panic.

A resilient culture weathers problems better and experiences fewer stress-related breakdowns.

15.18 Warning Signs That Intervention Is Needed

Sometimes stress management methods are not enough, and professional help is warranted:

- **Severe Behavioral Changes**: A top performer becomes withdrawn, aggressive, or shows big personality shifts.
- **Constant Absences**: Frequent sick days or late arrivals might indicate serious burnout or anxiety.
- **Visible Physical Decline**: Extreme weight changes, perpetual exhaustion, or signs of substance misuse.
- **Alarming Comments**: References to giving up, hopelessness, or other signs of deep distress.
- **Team Impact**: Widespread negativity, conflicts, or dropping performance across multiple employees.

Do not ignore these signals. A private discussion and referral to expert support could save someone's well-being—and possibly their life.

15.19 Long-Term Benefits of Managing Stress and Preventing Burnout

Investing in stress prevention is not just "nice to have":

- **Better Retention**: Employees stay where they feel cared for, reducing turnover costs.
- **Increased Engagement**: People who feel balanced perform with more creativity and efficiency.
- **Healthy Team Spirit**: Less conflict arises when everyone is not on edge.
- **Positive Brand Image**: Job candidates often research company culture. A workplace known for balanced expectations attracts strong talent.
- **Sustainable Growth**: Leaders can guide consistently when they are not constantly exhausted or firefighting crises.

Over time, a calm yet focused environment boosts productivity and human satisfaction.

15.20 Conclusion of Chapter 15

Stress is unavoidable in a dynamic workplace, but burnout should not be seen as a normal cost of doing business. Through thoughtful scheduling, open communication, balanced workloads, and genuine care, bosses can shield themselves and their employees from the worst effects of relentless pressure. Small efforts—like mindful pauses, clear role definitions, or flexible arrangements—add up to a major difference in mental well-being. By tackling stress systematically, you build a team that is healthier, happier, and equipped to tackle challenges with steady confidence.

Chapter 16: Inspiring Innovation and Creativity

In a rapidly shifting marketplace, creativity and innovation are vital for staying relevant. Many bosses focus on routines and risk-avoidance, which can stifle fresh thinking. However, the best leaders recognize that to stand out—whether through new products, efficient processes, or imaginative branding—they must foster a culture where innovative ideas flourish. This chapter offers practical methods for unleashing creativity in your team, moving beyond clichés about "thinking outside the box" and into concrete techniques that yield real breakthroughs.

16.1 Why Innovation Matters

1. **Competitive Edge**: Novel products or services attract customers, distinguishing you from rivals.
2. **Efficiency Gains**: Streamlined methods or new technologies can cut costs and improve outcomes.
3. **Employee Engagement**: People often find creative tasks more meaningful, boosting job satisfaction.
4. **Adaptation to Change**: Industries evolve. Innovation lets you shift gears quickly.
5. **Long-Term Survival**: Companies that fail to innovate risk being left behind by more agile competitors.

Rather than wait for a crisis, forward-thinking bosses cultivate creativity proactively.

16.2 Overcoming Barriers to Creativity

Despite its importance, creativity can be blocked by common pitfalls:

1. **Fear of Mistakes**: If staff fear blame, they will not propose bold ideas.
2. **Rigid Hierarchy**: Creative thoughts are stifled when only top executives can make decisions.

3. **Excessive Workload**: Overworked employees have no mental room to explore new concepts.
4. **Traditional Mindsets**: Phrases like "We have always done it this way" dismiss fresh perspectives.
5. **Overemphasis on Immediate Returns**: Innovation can be unpredictable and might not yield results overnight. Constant short-term focus smothers long-term thinking.

Tackling these barriers paves the way for a more open, imaginative environment.

16.3 Setting the Stage for Innovation

1. **Articulate a Clear Purpose**: Show how creativity supports bigger goals, such as entering a new market or improving customer satisfaction.
2. **Encourage Questions**: Let staff know it is fine—even encouraged—to question processes or challenge assumptions.
3. **Safe-to-Fail Experiments**: Create small pilot projects where risks are limited, allowing employees to try new ideas without fear of massive losses.
4. **Provide Resources**: People need time, tools, and sometimes budgets to experiment. If everything is allocated to routine tasks, innovation stalls.
5. **Open-Door Policies**: Signal that anyone can share an idea, no matter their rank.

A supportive climate where employees know innovation is valued lays the groundwork for breakthroughs.

16.4 Structuring Brainstorm Sessions

One of the most common ways to spark creativity is the brainstorming meeting, but many are run poorly:

- **Focus the Topic**: Clearly define the problem or goal. Vague prompts like "Let's brainstorm ways to improve everything" lead nowhere.
- **Set Ground Rules**: No judgment or criticism during idea generation; keep the atmosphere positive and free-flowing.

- **Time Limit**: Brainstorming should be concise—often 15-30 minutes—so energy stays high.
- **Diverse Team**: Mix people from different departments or backgrounds to combine varied perspectives.
- **Harvest Ideas**: After the session, categorize and refine them. Follow up quickly so people see that the best suggestions get traction.

With discipline and structure, brainstorming can yield a wealth of inventive ideas.

16.5 Leveraging Cross-Functional Collaboration

Innovation often happens when people with different expertise work together:

1. **Project Swaps**: Periodically let employees spend time in another department to learn fresh approaches.
2. **Task Forces**: Assemble small groups from finance, marketing, product design, etc. to tackle a specific challenge.
3. **Shared Tools**: Use project management platforms accessible to all relevant teams so they can track each other's progress and contribute insights.
4. **Communication Bridges**: Hold regular cross-team briefings where departments present updates, inviting feedback from outside their usual circles.

Cross-pollination of ideas frequently leads to creative leaps that departmental silos block.

16.6 Balancing Freedom and Guidance

An overly strict environment kills creativity, but complete absence of direction can cause chaos. Strive for equilibrium:

- **Flexible Goals**: Offer a general target—like cutting production costs by 10%—but let the team decide how.

- **Set Constraints**: Define budget limits, timelines, or quality standards so people innovate within realistic boundaries.
- **Mentoring**: Pair employees with experienced leaders who can offer feedback without micromanaging.
- **Periodic Check-Ins**: Rather than daily oversight, hold brief milestone reviews to ensure progress is on track.

Clear frameworks with enough leeway encourage thoughtful experimentation.

16.7 Encouraging a "Prototype and Test" Mindset

Prolonged analysis or endless meetings drain creative momentum. A better approach is quick prototyping:

1. **Build Small Versions**: Whether it is a draft design, a mock interface, or a scaled-down pilot, create something tangible fast.
2. **Test with Real Users**: Gather feedback from customers or internal stakeholders early.
3. **Iterate Quickly**: Refine the prototype based on responses. This loop repeats until you reach a viable solution.
4. **Fail Fast**: If an idea shows little promise, learn what you can and move on before major resources are spent.

This cyclical method can spark more creativity than theoretical discussions that never produce results.

16.8 Using Technology Tools for Idea Management

Modern software helps track and refine ideas:

- **Idea Voting Platforms**: Tools where employees can post suggestions and coworkers can upvote or comment.
- **Innovation Portals**: Central places for storing prototypes, user feedback, and analytics, so nothing gets lost.
- **Project Collaboration**: Applications like Slack or Microsoft Teams let cross-functional members discuss creative insights in real time.

- **Online Workshops**: Virtual whiteboards and brainstorming apps support distributed teams, capturing random thoughts that might blossom into major developments.

By organizing the creative process digitally, you reduce the risk of losing brilliant insights in email threads or meeting notes.

16.9 Cultivating an Open Mindset in Staff

Creativity flourishes when individuals believe their input is valued:

1. **Celebrate Attempts**: Do not punish people if an idea does not pan out. Emphasize what the team learned.
2. **Offer Training**: Courses on design thinking, problem-solving frameworks, or creative techniques can sharpen everyone's inventive side.
3. **Promote Curiosity**: Urge staff to explore trends in other fields. Great ideas often come from transferring knowledge across industries.
4. **Recognize Curiosity Champions**: When someone leads the way in exploring new directions, highlight their inquisitive spirit as an example.

By nurturing an open-minded approach, employees remain eager to share fresh concepts.

16.10 Avoiding Micromanagement in Creative Projects

Creativity needs room to breathe, but some bosses worry about losing control:

- **Set Clear Outcomes, Not Detailed Steps**: If you specify each step, you crush spontaneity and imagination.
- **Trust the Team**: If you hired skilled people, let them figure out how best to meet the goal.
- **Provide Mentoring, Not Control**: Offer expertise or resources but do not overshadow them with constant direction.
- **Accept a Bit of Chaos**: Early creative stages can look messy. Resist the urge to tidy up too quickly; sometimes the best ideas emerge from this mess.

Loosening the reins can feel uncomfortable, but it is often necessary for true innovation.

16.11 Recognizing and Rewarding Creative Wins

As covered in the previous chapter, recognition matters. The same principles apply to creativity:

1. **Publicly Commend Efforts**: During company meetings or in newsletters, mention the team or individual behind a breakthrough idea.
2. **Highlight Original Thinking**: Specifically praise the inventive aspect, not just the end result, so people see that fresh angles are appreciated.
3. **Offer Meaningful Rewards**: Perhaps let them lead the next big project or attend an industry conference.
4. **Document Success Stories**: Keep a record of successful ideas and their impact to inspire others.

This approach cements creativity as a valued component of your culture.

16.12 Looking Outside the Organization for Inspiration

Sometimes, teams get stuck in their own routines. External perspectives can reignite creativity:

- **Industry Benchmarking**: Study how top competitors solve similar problems.
- **Customer Panels**: Invite a small group of loyal or challenging customers to share feedback or brainstorm with the team.
- **Academic Tie-Ins**: Collaborate with research institutions or sponsor design contests at local colleges, benefiting from fresh academic viewpoints.
- **Professional Associations**: Attend events or committees that connect you with peers from diverse backgrounds, exposing you to new methods.

Fresh viewpoints and partnerships can give your team an injection of ideas that might not arise internally.

16.13 Leading by Example: A Boss's Creativity

Your own behavior sets the tone:

1. **Share Ideas Freely**: Even if some are half-baked, letting staff see your creative thought process encourages them to do the same.
2. **Ask Thought-Provoking Questions**: Challenge the team with "What if...?" or "Why not...?" queries to push them beyond safe assumptions.
3. **Admit Your Own Learning**: If you explore a new concept or skill, mention it. Show that growth and experimentation never stop, even at the top.
4. **Stay Curious**: Read widely, talk to experts outside your field, or attend workshops to expand your own horizons.

Employees watch how you handle fresh ideas—if you appear static, they might mirror that inertia.

16.14 Handling Risks and Failures Positively

Innovation involves uncertainty. Not every brainstorm results in success:

- **Risk Assessment**: Encourage employees to identify possible challenges early. This discipline avoids reckless gambles.
- **Scaled Trials**: Start small to limit damage if an idea fails.
- **Post-Mortems**: After a project wraps, analyze what went well and what failed. Avoid blaming individuals; focus on system improvements.
- **Spread Risk**: Do not bank everything on one massive gamble. A portfolio of smaller experiments can be safer and still yield game-changing breakthroughs.

Reframing failures as valuable lessons fosters a healthier environment that does not punish bold thinkers.

16.15 Creating an Innovation-Focused Environment

Beyond projects, shape a physical or virtual environment that fuels creativity:

- **Idea Walls**: A shared bulletin board (digital or physical) for random thoughts, sketches, or user feedback.
- **Creative Zones**: Areas free from interruptions where employees can think deeply or brainstorm in small groups.
- **Access to Tools**: Supply design software, prototyping kits, or data analytics platforms so employees can put ideas into practice easily.
- **Inspirational Material**: Display industry trends, success stories, or relevant data visuals around the office to spark new angles of thought.

Small environmental tweaks often yield significant boosts in creative output.

16.16 Encouraging Ongoing Learning

Innovation hinges on knowledge:

1. **Training Programs**: Regular workshops, online courses, or in-house seminars on cutting-edge topics.
2. **Reading Circles**: Groups of staff who read books or articles, then discuss them to generate new approaches.
3. **Guest Speakers**: Invite experts from other fields to share insights. A robotics specialist might inspire fresh solutions in a logistics team, for instance.
4. **Funding Experimentation**: Set aside a budget for employees to attend conferences or buy materials related to new ideas.

A learning-oriented culture ensures your workforce stays current and can adapt to emerging opportunities.

16.17 Balancing Short-Term Demands with Long-Term Vision

Leaders often get bogged down in daily tasks, leaving little space for visionary planning:

- **Reserve Creative Time**: Block segments for strategic thinking or concept exploration, free from routine demands.

- **Assign "Innovation Owners"**: Specific people tasked with scanning future market trends, new tech, or potential partnerships.
- **Bridge the Gap**: Translate big visions into smaller pilot projects that can run alongside everyday operations.
- **Communicate Vision**: Let the entire team know the long-term directions so they can propose relevant ideas.

By balancing present efficiency with future possibilities, you reduce the risk of stagnation.

16.18 Inclusion and Diversity as Catalysts

Diverse teams generate more varied ideas. A homogenous group may unknowingly limit its own perspective:

1. **Hire from Different Backgrounds**: Seek out individuals who have varied experiences, skill sets, or cultural viewpoints.
2. **Inclusive Brainstorm Protocol**: Make sure quieter voices get equal time to share. Dominant personalities can overshadow fresh insights.
3. **Rotation of Meeting Leaders**: Sometimes let junior employees or those from different departments facilitate sessions, balancing power dynamics.
4. **Respect Varied Thinking Styles**: Some employees prefer visuals, others prefer data. Provide multiple channels for idea expression.

When employees see their uniqueness is valued, they feel safer contributing original thoughts.

16.19 Monitoring and Measuring Innovative Efforts

While creativity is often subjective, certain metrics or observations can show progress:

- **Number of Ideas Submitted**: Track how many suggestions the team puts forth, though quality matters more than quantity.
- **Pilot Projects Launched**: How many experiments are in motion at a given time, and do they align with strategic goals?

- **Implementation Rate**: Of all the proposals, how many move to execution or further development?
- **Financial or Market Impact**: Over time, measure whether new ideas lead to improved revenue, cost savings, or brand visibility.
- **Employee Feedback**: Surveys can reveal whether staff feel empowered to propose new concepts.

Just be careful not to turn creativity into a rigid numbers game—use these metrics as guideposts, not absolute measures.

16.20 Conclusion of Chapter 16

Inspiring innovation is not a one-time event but an ongoing process that calls for leadership commitment. By carving out safe spaces for trial and error, encouraging cross-functional collaboration, balancing freedom with structure, and valuing diverse perspectives, you can unlock a wellspring of new ideas. The path to creativity involves risk, but the rewards—whether in fresh products, improved efficiencies, or happier staff—are invaluable. As you continue leading with a creative mindset, the organization can evolve in ways that keep it ahead of changing markets.

Next, we will look at decision-making techniques for leaders. Even the most innovative teams need solid frameworks for making choices. With numerous ideas and paths available, understanding how to evaluate and select the best course is critical. By combining creativity with smart decision processes, you form a powerful blend that both sparks fresh possibilities and guides them toward fruitful outcomes.

Chapter 17: Decision-Making Techniques for Leaders

A boss constantly faces decisions—small, medium, and large. Some are routine and quick, while others carry serious weight for business direction, staff well-being, or financial health. Decision-making can seem overwhelming if you lack a clear approach. This chapter outlines a range of practical methods to guide your thinking, reduce errors, and ensure choices align with strategic goals. From analytical tools to collaborative methods, you will gain insights that boost your confidence when making tough calls.

17.1 Why Decision-Making Skills Are Vital

1. **Efficiency**: Solid decision-making prevents delays that stall progress. Confusion often arises when a leader hesitates or changes course too often.
2. **Team Confidence**: Employees feel more secure and motivated under a boss who makes stable, logical decisions. Inconsistent or unclear choices create tension.
3. **Resource Allocation**: Many decisions involve how to distribute limited funds or manpower. Good judgment ensures the best possible use of these resources.
4. **Strategic Direction**: A business's success hinges on setting the right direction. Misguided choices can waste years of effort and open the door to competitors.
5. **Risk Management**: A well-thought-out process can spot hidden dangers early, minimizing potential harm.

Leaders who handle decisions with care set a positive tone for the entire workplace.

17.2 Common Decision Pitfalls

Before exploring deeper into structured methods, let us examine common mistakes that undermine decisions:

1. **Emotional Impulses**: Acting purely on feelings—like anger, fear, or excitement—can lead to regrettable outcomes if not balanced with rational data.
2. **Analysis Paralysis**: Gathering endless data without forming conclusions wastes time. While research is necessary, leaders must know when to stop and choose.
3. **Confirmation Bias**: People often favor facts supporting an initial opinion, ignoring evidence that suggests another path.
4. **Groupthink**: Teams may push for unanimity by downplaying risks or failing to question assumptions. In these cases, diverse viewpoints get drowned out.
5. **Ignoring Long-Term Impacts**: Focusing only on short-term gains can create bigger challenges later.

Recognizing these traps helps you stay alert and steer the decision-making process away from pitfalls.

17.3 Rational vs. Intuitive Approaches

Two broad styles often shape how people make choices:

- **Rational/Analytical**: Collect data, compare options, use logic. This style suits complex, high-stakes decisions that demand thoroughness. However, it can be slow and might overlook unquantifiable factors.
- **Intuitive**: Rely on past experiences, instincts, or gut feelings. This can be fast and works well for everyday, low-risk decisions where a boss's expertise provides strong guidance. But purely intuitive moves can be flawed if personal biases or emotions cloud judgment.

A balanced leader knows when to apply each style—sometimes blending them—to address different challenges effectively.

17.4 The Classic "Pros and Cons" List

This simple method remains a favorite for its clarity:

1. **List the Options**: Write down each potential path.
2. **Identify Positives and Negatives**: Under each option, note advantages and disadvantages.
3. **Weigh Importance**: Some pros or cons matter more than others. You might give them a numerical rating if you want to be more precise.
4. **Compare Overall Results**: Identify which choice offers the strongest positives with the fewest serious negatives.
5. **Double Check**: See if any important element is missing.

While basic, the pros-and-cons tool forces you to think systematically about each choice.

17.5 The 5 Whys Technique

Commonly used for root-cause analysis, the 5 Whys can also guide decisions:

1. **State the Problem or Choice**: For example, "Should we delay the product launch?"
2. **Ask Why Repeatedly**: Each answer spurs the next "why," digging into underlying issues.
3. **Uncover True Motivation or Obstacle**: Maybe the real reason you consider delaying is that the design team lacks some critical data.
4. **Inform Your Choice**: Once you see the core reason for hesitation, you can address it directly instead of treating symptoms.

By clarifying root issues, the 5 Whys often lead to more confident decisions.

17.6 Cost-Benefit Analysis

For financial or resource-based decisions, cost-benefit analysis offers a structured approach:

1. **Define Variables**: List all expected costs (money, time, staff hours) and potential benefits (revenue, brand growth, efficiency gains).
2. **Estimate Values**: Assign approximate dollar amounts or time measurements to each variable. This can be rough but should be realistic.

3. **Compare Ratios**: Calculate if the benefits significantly outweigh the costs or vice versa.
4. **Factor in Non-Quantifiable Elements**: Some benefits—like public goodwill—are hard to quantify. Consider them separately if needed.
5. **Assess Risk Range**: Possibly run a best-case, worst-case, and middle-case scenario.

If an option shows minimal gain or heavy costs, you might shift resources elsewhere. This method is especially helpful when budgets are tight and clarity is needed on financial payoffs.

17.7 The Decision Matrix (Weighted Criteria)

When many factors play a role, a decision matrix can help:

1. **List Choices**: Down one side, write possible options (e.g., different suppliers, marketing strategies, or hires).
2. **Define Criteria**: Across the top, note the variables like cost, reliability, speed, cultural fit, or long-term potential.
3. **Assign Weights**: Decide which criteria hold the most importance. For instance, cost might be 30%, reliability 20%, speed 20%, cultural fit 15%, and potential 15%.
4. **Rate Each Option**: Score them (perhaps 1–10) for every criterion.
5. **Calculate Weighted Totals**: Multiply each score by its weight and add up.
6. **Compare Results**: The highest total often indicates the strongest choice, but also review if the data makes sense.

A well-made matrix reduces guesswork and organizes complex details in an understandable format.

17.8 Thinking in Scenarios

Scenario planning helps leaders handle uncertainty:

1. **Identify Key Variables**: Focus on factors that strongly influence future outcomes (economy, technology shifts, competitor actions).

2. **Develop Plausible Scenarios**: For each variable, imagine different potential states—positive, neutral, negative. Combine them to create a handful of realistic future scenarios.
3. **Craft Responses**: If scenario A arises (tech evolves fast, competitor invests heavily), how will your team respond?
4. **Watch Real-World Indicators**: Monitor signals hinting at which scenario is coming to pass.
5. **Remain Flexible**: Plans may shift if a scenario changes. Keep your approach fluid.

This method is invaluable when decisions span years or depend on external factors beyond your control.

17.9 Group Decision Methods

While some decisions rest solely with the boss, involving others can lead to broader acceptance and stronger ideas:

1. **Consensus Building**: The group discusses until all members can accept a single option. This can take time but fosters unity.
2. **Majority Vote**: Fast and democratic, but minority voices may feel unheard. Works best for less critical matters.
3. **Nominal Group Technique**: Each member writes down suggestions privately, then they're shared and ranked. This reduces dominant personalities overshadowing quieter people.
4. **Delphi Method**: Collect anonymous feedback from experts in rounds, refining options until reaching a near-consensus. Useful for complex or specialized issues.

Knowing which group method suits the situation can improve both the quality and reception of your choices.

17.10 The Importance of Time Frames

Rushed decisions can overlook crucial data, while lengthy delays may lead to missed chances:

1. **Set a Deadline**: Even if flexible, mark a date by which you must choose. This prevents endless debate.
2. **Use Tiered Decision Speeds**: Minor decisions can be made in minutes or hours, while major ones might require days or weeks of analysis.
3. **Stay Aware of Opportunity Costs**: Delaying can be costly if a competitor acts sooner or if you lose a favorable deal.
4. **Plan for Revisions**: Some decisions benefit from a "preliminary call," followed by final confirmation after certain checks.

Time management in decision-making keeps the team moving and reduces the risk of becoming stuck.

17.11 The Role of Data and Expertise

In an age of big data, many leaders gather as many facts as possible. However, this is only helpful if used properly:

1. **Seek Quality Data**: Ensure sources are reliable and up-to-date. Old or biased data misleads.
2. **Combine Qualitative Insights**: Expert opinions or user testimonials can reveal truths hidden behind raw numbers.
3. **Stay Alert to Overload**: Limit your data set to what's truly relevant.
4. **Ask Experts Specific Questions**: If you consult a specialist, define your question clearly so they focus on your real concerns.

Balancing factual info with expert judgment leads to more robust conclusions.

17.12 Handling Complex Trade-Offs

Some decisions involve moral or ethical considerations, brand identity, or long-term environmental effects. For example, you might weigh cheaper production methods against pollution risks or brand damage. Methods to manage these trade-offs include:

- **Ethical Checklists**: Pose questions like "Could this harm vulnerable communities or employees?"

- **Stakeholder Impact**: Consider how each group—employees, customers, suppliers, community—would be affected.
- **Long-Term Reputation**: Might a short-term benefit undermine your standing in future years?
- **Legal and Compliance Factors**: Ensure no option violates regulations or company policies.

Weighing these qualitative factors can be tricky, but ignoring them can cause serious reputational or legal harm later.

17.13 Dealing with Uncertainty and Risk

Few decisions come with complete certainty. Leaders must manage risk actively:

1. **Risk Assessments**: Estimate the likelihood of negative outcomes and their potential severity.
2. **Mitigation Plans**: If a certain risk is high-impact, prepare steps to reduce the chance or lessen the damage if it happens.
3. **Contingency Funds**: Keep some budget or time buffer in case you need to correct course quickly.
4. **Test Runs**: Pilot programs can reveal hidden pitfalls before a full launch.
5. **Insurance**: In certain industries, insurance or hedging strategies can safeguard you financially.

Accepting that some risk is unavoidable while taking steps to control it is a hallmark of strong decision-making.

17.14 Communicating the Final Decision

Once a choice is made, how you present it can influence team morale:

- **Explain the Rationale**: Outline the reasoning without overwhelming detail. People should see how you weighed options.
- **Be Transparent About Downsides**: Acknowledge potential drawbacks, showing you did not ignore them.

- **Clarify Next Steps**: Assign responsibilities and timelines so the decision moves into action.
- **Invite Questions**: Staff may have concerns or need clarifications. Address them patiently to build trust.
- **Stay Consistent in Follow-Up**: If you pivot soon after announcing, explain why. Sudden reversals without reason cause confusion.

Clear, honest communication fosters acceptance and ensures everyone understands their role.

17.15 Reviewing Decisions After the Fact

Hindsight can be a valuable teacher. Conduct periodic reviews:

1. **Assess Outcomes**: Did the decision meet objectives? If not, why?
2. **Check Assumptions**: Many choices rely on forecasts. Compare them to actual results to see if your data was accurate.
3. **Spot Patterns**: If certain pitfalls appear repeatedly, update your process to avoid them.
4. **Document Lessons**: Summarize the experience for future reference. This helps new staff or managers learn from past calls.

A boss who routinely evaluates decisions grows more skilled at balancing risk, data, and intuition over time.

17.16 Empowering Others to Decide

You do not need to handle every decision yourself. In fact, delegating decisions can free your time and empower staff:

- **Define Decision Boundaries**: Let team members know which decisions they can make on their own.
- **Train and Support**: Provide guidelines, scenario examples, and mentorship so they feel confident.
- **Accept Mistakes**: If a team member errs, help them learn rather than punishing them. This fosters self-assuredness.

- **Check In, Don't Hover**: Periodic updates are fine, but micromanagement undercuts trust.
- **Reward Good Judgment**: Acknowledge staff who make strong calls that align with the organization's values.

Distributed decision-making can boost agility and engagement throughout the company.

17.17 Special Cases: Crisis Decisions

Emergencies—like data breaches or sudden revenue losses—test a boss's resolve:

1. **Shift to Rapid Mode**: Long analysis might be impossible. Use core data quickly while trusting expert counsel.
2. **Communicate Urgently**: Keep stakeholders updated, even if details are still emerging. This prevents rumors.
3. **Designate Roles**: In a crisis, confusion is fatal. Specify who handles communications, who fixes technical issues, etc.
4. **Focus on Priorities**: Control damage, protect employees and customers, then fix the root cause.
5. **Learn Post-Crisis**: After stabilizing, do a thorough review to avoid repeating the same problem.

Handling crises well shows strong leadership and can even improve team cohesion during tough times.

17.18 Ethical Dilemmas and Judgment

Leaders sometimes confront moral gray areas—e.g., should you adopt cost-cutting measures that could reduce staff jobs or wages? Approaches:

- **Consult a Moral or Legal Advisor**: Complex dilemmas may require ethical or legal expertise.
- **Balance Stakeholders**: Weigh how different groups are affected—customers, employees, shareholders.

- **Check Personal and Organizational Values**: Does the choice align with the character you want to exhibit as a leader?
- **Be Willing to Adjust**: If you learn new information that conflicts with your moral stance, reconsider the plan promptly.

Decisions in these spheres define your reputation and the trust level in your leadership.

17.19 Keeping Emotions and Ego in Check

A leader's feelings can cloud judgments or push them to defend a flawed choice:

- **Self-Awareness**: Recognize if pride or fear of looking weak is causing you to stick with a bad plan.
- **Invite Critique**: Encourage a trusted colleague to challenge your assumptions.
- **Use Calm Periods**: When tensions run high, consider waiting if possible, then revisit the issue with a clear mind.
- **Separate Personal Ties**: Do not let personal liking or dislike for someone overshadow objective merits of a proposal.

When you remain humble and self-aware, decisions become more rational and fair.

17.20 Conclusion of Chapter 17

Decision-making is the backbone of leadership. By blending structured methods such as cost-benefit analysis or scenario planning with a grounded sense of ethics and empathy, bosses can chart effective paths forward. Each approach—whether it is a simple pros-and-cons list or a complex weighted matrix—helps keep biases in check and ensures a transparent process. Communicating decisions well and reviewing outcomes later closes the loop, driving continuous growth in judgment.

Chapter 18: Managing Different Personalities and Work Styles

A typical workplace brings together individuals with varied backgrounds, temperaments, and methods of getting tasks done. Some staff members are outgoing and thrive on group projects, while others prefer quiet, focused sessions alone. Some might think in precise data terms, whereas others rely on emotions and intuition. As a boss, you face the challenge of aligning these varied personalities toward shared objectives without stifling their natural strengths. This chapter explains how to identify and adapt to different work styles, promote harmony, and keep your team unified despite personal differences.

18.1 Why Personality Differences Matter

1. **Communication Gaps**: A direct person might clash with someone who is sensitive to blunt remarks.
2. **Task Preferences**: Certain employees excel at detailed planning, while others shine in creative brainstorming.
3. **Conflict Risk**: Strong-willed personalities can struggle if they lack strategies for compromise.
4. **Productivity Variations**: Understanding each individual's peak times and comfort zones can boost efficiency.
5. **Team Synergy**: When guided properly, diversity in personalities can lead to well-rounded solutions.

A boss who acknowledges these differences is better prepared to harness everyone's potential.

18.2 Recognizing Basic Personality Traits

While no label fits every nuance, leaders can note common personality dimensions:

- **Extroverted vs. Introverted**: Extroverts often speak up in meetings, enjoy social engagement, and process thoughts aloud. Introverts may reflect deeply before speaking and prefer written communication or smaller group settings.
- **Logical vs. Emotional**: Some staff reason mostly with data and logic, while others rely on their feelings or the group's mood.
- **Structured vs. Flexible**: Detail-oriented people like set plans and deadlines, whereas flexible types adapt spontaneously.
- **Collaborative vs. Independent**: Certain employees thrive in team activities, while others are happier handling tasks solo.

Observing these traits helps you adapt interactions and assignments for optimal outcomes.

18.3 Conducting Informal Assessments

You do not need to run formal personality tests to learn about people's work styles. Simple steps include:

1. **Observe Day-to-Day Behavior**: Note who volunteers for group projects, who hesitates to share thoughts publicly, or who meticulously organizes their tasks.
2. **Ask Open-Ended Questions**: During one-on-ones, inquire about how they prefer to receive feedback, their favorite project types, or which conditions help them focus.
3. **Watch Interactions**: Notice tension or synergy between staff members with opposing or complementary traits.
4. **Review Past Work**: Employees' success in prior assignments can hint at their strengths—analytical tasks, people-focused roles, or creative challenges.

Armed with this knowledge, you can fine-tune how you lead each person.

18.4 Balancing Extroverts and Introverts

Extroverts bring energy and quick collaboration, while introverts offer calm analysis and depth. Tips to handle both:

- **Meeting Formats**: Provide an agenda ahead of time so introverts can prepare. Then, give them moments to speak without extroverts dominating.
- **Equal Voice**: If an extrovert hogs the floor, gently redirect to quieter members. For introverts, encourage them to share their written thoughts or hold smaller group discussions.
- **Task Distribution**: Put extroverts in roles needing frequent interaction, like client relations, if they excel at it. Let introverts focus on detailed research or tasks requiring deep concentration.
- **Respect Downtime**: Introverts often recharge alone, so avoid scheduling back-to-back group events. Extroverts may prefer to gather during lunch or breaks.

By honoring both styles, you create an environment where each group can thrive.

18.5 Handling Analytical vs. Emotional Thinkers

A person who relies on data might find emotional arguments unconvincing, and vice versa. Approaches:

1. **Mix Logic and Empathy**: When presenting decisions, share both factual evidence (numbers, case studies) and human considerations (employee morale, client feelings).
2. **Validate Each Approach**: Assure data-minded individuals that feelings do matter, while also showing emotional thinkers that facts shape balanced solutions.
3. **Pair Them on Projects**: A data specialist and an empathetic communicator can form a powerful duo—one ensures accuracy, the other fosters user-friendly outcomes.
4. **Manage Conflicts**: If a debate arises, remind both sides that the best choice often merges logical proof with people-friendly insights.

Encouraging mutual respect keeps the team from splitting into separate camps.

18.6 Matching Structured vs. Flexible Styles

Some employees want clear schedules and deadlines, while others work best with loose outlines:

- **Project Timelines**: Offer standard milestones for those who crave structure. Also, let flexible folks propose alternative routes if it yields equal or better results.
- **Defined Roles**: A detailed person might handle scheduling or quality checks, while a more adaptable teammate tackles surprises or last-minute changes.
- **Check-In Frequency**: Highly organized individuals may appreciate frequent progress updates, whereas flexible ones might prefer a bit more independence between check-ins.
- **Accept Different Methods**: As long as both types meet quality standards, do not force them into a single mold.

Blending structure with adaptability fosters both consistency and innovation.

18.7 Encouraging Collaborative vs. Independent Workers

Not everyone is suited to constant group assignments. Methods to satisfy both:

1. **Balanced Project Assignments**: Include some tasks that require team efforts and some that can be done solo.
2. **Team-Based Goals**: Even for independent tasks, highlight the shared purpose, so lone workers still sense a collective mission.
3. **Individual Accountability**: In group settings, define each person's piece to avoid frustration for those who prefer self-directed work.
4. **Small Collaboration Groups**: Large committees can overwhelm individuals who prefer autonomy. Pair or trio structures might work better for them.

A careful mix of group and solo tasks keeps everyone in their best zone.

18.8 Communicating with Different Personalities

Effective bosses adapt communication style:

- **Direct vs. Indirect**: Some employees appreciate blunt feedback, while others react poorly to harsh wording. Use a gentler tone where needed.
- **Written vs. Verbal**: Certain staff understand ideas best through written outlines, whereas others grasp them faster through face-to-face talks.
- **Details vs. Summaries**: Detail-oriented people want in-depth specifics. Big-picture thinkers prefer an overview with key points.
- **Cultural Factors**: In global teams, some cultures value polite phrasing or indirect suggestions, while others expect straightforward talk.

Adapting to these preferences ensures clarity and prevents misunderstandings that come from one-size-fits-all messaging.

18.9 Conflict Resolution and Personality Clashes

Differences can spark tension. A boss who understands personalities can mediate effectively:

1. **Identify Root Causes**: Is the issue about style (e.g., direct talk vs. sensitive reaction) or actual job responsibilities?
2. **Encourage Empathy**: Have each person describe their viewpoint and show them how others might see the same situation differently.
3. **Set Behavioral Guidelines**: If someone's strong tone offends others, agree on how to phrase feedback with respect.
4. **Use Common Goals**: Remind conflicting parties of the team's bigger objective. This perspective often dissolves petty disputes.
5. **Private Mediation**: Handle serious tension behind closed doors, giving each person a fair chance to share without public embarrassment.

Resolving clashes swiftly prevents deeper divisions and maintains team harmony.

18.10 Building Unity While Respecting Uniqueness

It is possible to unify the group while letting individuals retain their personal flair:

- **Team Charter**: Work together to define core values—respect, fairness, collaboration. Everyone agrees to uphold them.
- **Celebrate Strengths**: Acknowledge how different traits contribute to success. People feel appreciated when their style is seen as an asset, not a problem.
- **Rotate Roles**: Sometimes let a structured person lead a creative project, or an extrovert handle data tasks, to stretch their capacities.
- **Foster Shared Rituals**: Periodic gatherings or routines that everyone can join—like monthly skill-sharing sessions—build a sense of belonging.

When done respectfully, collective bonding and personal authenticity can coexist.

18.11 Delegation Based on Personality

A boss who knows each person's temperament can delegate tasks that match (or challenge) them:

1. **Compatible Assignments**: Place a detail-loving individual in charge of budgets, a sociable one on client outreach, etc.
2. **Balance Growth**: Occasionally assign tasks outside someone's comfort zone so they develop broader skills.
3. **Avoid Pigeonholing**: Do not always funnel the same tasks to the same people. This can lead to boredom and block growth.
4. **Communication of Rationale**: Explain why you chose a certain person for a role, highlighting their strengths. This boosts confidence.

Delegation is not just about offloading work—it is about strategic fit that maximizes both efficiency and personal development.

18.12 Leading Multi-Generational Teams

Modern workplaces often blend older employees with younger staff who bring different norms:

- **Value Experience**: Older staff's historical knowledge can guide decisions. Let them mentor less-experienced members.
- **Recognize New Skills**: Younger workers might excel in digital tools or social media. Encourage them to teach others.
- **Flexible Communication**: Some employees prefer phone calls or in-person chats, others rely on instant messaging or email. Accept these differences where possible.
- **Respect All Contributions**: Avoid stereotypes like "older people resist change" or "younger folks are too impatient." Focus on individual capabilities.

Intergenerational synergy can produce innovative perspectives and stable continuity if managed well.

18.13 Remote Work Styles and Personalities

With more remote or hybrid arrangements, personality traits may show up differently:

1. **Introverts Might Thrive**: Working from home can provide the quiet they need. However, they might feel more isolated.
2. **Extroverts May Feel Stifled**: They often crave social contact. Encourage virtual coffee breaks or video calls.
3. **Monitoring Work**: Balanced oversight is needed. Micro-managing remote staff erodes trust, but too little contact can cause miscommunication.
4. **Online Collaboration Tools**: Provide digital platforms where everyone can communicate effectively without crowding personal space.
5. **Check Emotional Tone**: In emails or chats, words can seem harsher than intended. Encourage polite language and clarify potential misunderstandings.

Adapting leadership to remote personalities helps sustain productivity and group morale.

18.14 Using Personality Frameworks Carefully

Some organizations use tools like Myers-Briggs or DiSC. While they offer insights, they are not foolproof:

- **Avoid Labeling**: Do not reduce someone to a four-letter type or single label. Real individuals are more nuanced.
- **Focus on Awareness**: These models can spark conversations about strengths or communication preferences.
- **Stay Flexible**: People grow over time. A test result from five years ago might not reflect current behavior.
- **Use as a Starting Point**: Let the tool guide initial discussions, then observe actual interactions to refine your understanding.

When used responsibly, frameworks help build mutual understanding without boxing anyone in.

18.15 Encouraging Mutual Respect Among Different Styles

A boss can shape the team culture to value differences:

1. **Highlight Success Stories**: Show times when a creative thinker solved a unique problem, or a detail-oriented person saved the day through rigorous checking.
2. **Model Respect**: When someone with a different style speaks up, listen attentively. Your example can set the tone for the entire group.
3. **Curb Sarcasm or Mockery**: Joking about someone's quietness or over-excitability can hurt trust. Step in if you notice teasing.
4. **Group Acknowledgments**: Mention in meetings how each approach—logical, empathetic, structured, flexible—made a difference.

This environment invites people to be themselves without fear of being sidelined.

18.16 Mentoring and Pairing Strategies

Sometimes pairing employees with complementary personalities strengthens the team:

- **Mentoring Newcomers**: A calm, experienced mentor can help an energetic but inexperienced new hire channel their enthusiasm productively.
- **Expert-Noob Partnerships**: A senior analyst (logical) might join forces with a more creative junior staffer to produce balanced solutions.
- **Peer Coaching**: Two employees with opposite work habits can teach each other how to manage time or how to generate fresh ideas.
- **Rotation of Pairs**: Change pairings over time, so employees learn from diverse partners.

Such cross-fertilization fosters a learning culture and reduces tension born of misunderstandings.

18.17 Handling the Strong-Willed or Challenging Personalities

Sometimes, a person's style is particularly forceful or abrasive. Steps:

1. **Clarify Behavioral Expectations**: Explain the difference between being assertive and being disrespectful.
2. **Coach Private Communication**: If they overshadow others in meetings, speak privately and set limits on how much they dominate.
3. **Redirect Energy**: Strong-willed individuals can excel in roles needing decisive action, so long as they respect collaboration.
4. **Involve HR if Needed**: If repeated warnings do not help, official performance plans or disciplinary measures might be necessary.

This approach maintains fairness and ensures one difficult individual does not derail team spirit.

18.18 Supporting Shy or Less Assertive Team Members

Those who speak less may have valuable insights that remain hidden:

- **Ask for Written Input**: They might express ideas better in writing. Provide that option.
- **Call on Them Gently**: In meetings, invite their viewpoint without putting them on the spot in a stressful manner.
- **Praise Small Contributions**: Point out how their quiet but thoughtful remarks helped, boosting their confidence.
- **Offer Safe Spaces**: Consider smaller breakout groups or one-on-one sessions for idea-sharing before a large gathering.

By creating a supportive setting, you can unlock the potential of quieter staff who might otherwise remain overlooked.

18.19 Measuring Team Harmony and Output

Is the combination of different personalities yielding positive results? Key checks:

- **Team Feedback**: Periodic surveys or informal chats can reveal satisfaction levels with interactions, clarity of roles, and perceived fairness.
- **Turnover Rates**: High turnover sometimes signals unresolved personality clashes or poor cultural fit.
- **Conflict Frequency**: Occasional disagreements are normal, but constant friction suggests an issue with communication or role alignment.
- **Performance Metrics**: If projects frequently meet goals while staff remain engaged, you are likely balancing styles well.
- **Observing Collaboration Quality**: Do people ask each other for help? Is knowledge shared freely?

A healthy team harnesses differences in style to achieve strong outcomes with minimal drama.

18.20 Conclusion of Chapter 18

Managing different personalities and work styles is both an art and a science. It demands awareness of each individual's traits, careful communication, and a flexible approach to delegation and conflict resolution. A boss who welcomes these differences—turning them into strengths—will see a boost in creativity, morale, and overall performance. By balancing extroverts with introverts, logical with emotional thinkers, structured with flexible planners, and collaborative with independent workers, you shape a workplace where people feel respected and productive.

Next, we will look at building a legacy of strong leadership that outlasts your direct involvement. Once you master working with diverse personalities, the next step is establishing systems, values, and structures that remain effective even as teams change or as you move on to higher roles. This ensures that the positive environment you foster endures well into the future.

Chapter 19: Building a Legacy of Strong Leadership

Once you have honed the daily methods of guiding a team—through clarity, fairness, and strategic thinking—you also have to think about the larger mark you leave behind. Leading a project or a department for a few years is one thing; creating a lasting, positive impact is another. A legacy of strong leadership persists even when you step away or change roles. People still benefit from the values and systems you put in place, continuing the path of progress. This chapter shows how to construct that legacy by shaping culture, nurturing future leaders, and embedding principles that stand the test of time.

19.1 Defining Legacy in Leadership

Legacy is not about personal fame. Instead, it involves:

1. **Sustainable Systems**: Processes that continue working smoothly long after your departure.
2. **Healthy Culture**: A set of shared behaviors and values your team adopts and upholds.
3. **Developed People**: Individuals you have guided who can lead effectively on their own.
4. **Positive Brand**: A reputation for reliability and fairness that endures, attracting new talent and clients.
5. **Long-Lasting Goals**: Strategic objectives that remain relevant and keep progress rolling.

Leaders who think ahead about these elements set the stage for a lasting footprint rather than short-lived gains.

19.2 Why a Lasting Legacy Matters

1. **Company Stability**: An organization with strong systems and internal leadership is less vulnerable to sudden changes or crises.
2. **Talent Retention**: Employees are more likely to stay if they feel they are part of a larger mission with strong principles, rather than just short-term tasks.

3. **Efficiency**: Documented and repeatable practices reduce confusion, cutting down on the need to reinvent the wheel.
4. **Personal Fulfillment**: Many leaders want to know their efforts made a meaningful difference over time.
5. **Community Impact**: In some cases, your leadership legacy extends beyond the company, affecting local communities or industries.

By focusing on legacy, you ensure your leadership efforts extend well beyond daily demands.

19.3 Shaping Organizational Culture

Culture is the invisible glue that guides how people behave. Leaders who want to leave a mark need to:

- **Clarify Core Values**: Identify a handful of key principles, like integrity, respect, customer-focus, or innovation.
- **Model These Values**: Demonstrate them daily—if you promote honesty, be transparent. If you talk about respect, treat others kindly under pressure.
- **Align Policies**: Everything from hiring and promotion to rewards should match the stated values. If there is a mismatch, credibility suffers.
- **Encourage Storytelling**: Share real examples of employees who showed the core values. Let these success stories spread, reinforcing what matters.
- **Stay Consistent**: Shifting your stance on values confuses people. Stay anchored, even when it is tough.

A well-defined culture reduces internal friction and stands firm when external conditions shift.

19.4 Documenting Processes and Knowledge

Leaders often carry a wealth of expertise in their heads. If they leave without recording it, the team loses valuable insights. Steps to avoid this:

1. **Standard Operating Procedures (SOPs)**: Write clear instructions for repeated tasks or responsibilities. Update them over time.
2. **Knowledge Handover**: When someone is promoted or moves to another role, require a handover document explaining key contacts, resources, and steps.
3. **Wiki or Portal**: Keep an internal system where employees can add or revise instructions, tips, or best practices.
4. **Mentoring Sessions**: Senior employees can mentor newer staff, sharing knowledge in a structured way.
5. **Check for Gaps**: Periodically review if certain processes or decisions are still undocumented, plugging holes before they become issues.

This makes it easier for future leaders to step in and maintain continuity.

19.5 Grooming Future Leaders

A crucial element of a leadership legacy is how well you prepare the next wave of managers:

- **Identify Potential**: Spot employees who show skill at motivating peers, handling problems calmly, or thinking strategically.
- **Provide Opportunities**: Let them lead small projects or represent the department in cross-functional meetings.
- **Share Decision-Making**: Involve them in important choices, explaining your thought process.
- **Offer Training**: Formal courses or workshops can fill in gaps, from presentation skills to advanced problem-solving.
- **Encourage Self-Reflection**: Have them set their own goals, then discuss progress during regular one-on-ones.

Building new leaders within the organization prevents a vacuum when top-level people move on.

19.6 Avoiding Overdependence on One Person

Sometimes a dynamic boss becomes the sole problem-solver or main decision-maker, leaving the team helpless in their absence. To avoid that:

1. **Delegate**: Spread responsibilities widely, letting others gain competence and confidence.
2. **Teach vs. Just Tell**: Explain the "why" behind your decisions. This helps staff learn the process, not just the result.
3. **Encourage Collaboration**: If many staff members contribute to solutions, knowledge is shared rather than stuck in one person's mind.
4. **Rotate Roles**: Let employees temporarily handle new tasks so multiple individuals understand different parts of the operation.
5. **Create a Leadership Team**: If you have direct reports, empower them to handle key duties, forming a strong management layer.

This approach ensures that the entire operation does not crumble if one individual departs or takes leave.

19.7 Setting Clear Long-Term Goals

A leadership legacy includes objectives that outlive short projects. Steps to define them:

- **Link to Core Values**: If your values emphasize customer care, a long-term goal might be establishing the highest customer satisfaction in the market.
- **Think in Phases**: Break big ambitions into 3-year, 5-year, or 10-year targets so the path becomes clearer.
- **Involve the Team**: Let employees propose ideas. Shared ownership of big goals strengthens commitment.
- **Track Progress**: Check milestones periodically. Note achievements or revise targets if the environment changes.
- **Maintain Flexibility**: The business landscape shifts. Long-term goals should adapt without losing their core intent.

These goals serve as a guiding star, helping your successors align efforts with a larger direction you set in motion.

19.8 Building Ethical and Sustainable Practices

Leaders with a long view know that shortcuts can harm reputation or trust in the future. Thus:

1. **Adopt Ethical Standards**: Make sure contracts, hiring, and partner relations meet moral guidelines. No short-term profit is worth legal trouble or brand damage.
2. **Promote Accountability**: Ensure employees report wrongdoing, and handle it swiftly. A transparent process signals you take ethics seriously.
3. **Consider Environmental and Social Impact**: Depending on your industry, plan how to reduce waste or support local communities.
4. **Stay Within Compliance**: Regulations can be complex, but ignoring them can lead to fines or worse.
5. **Lead by Example**: A boss known for fairness sets the moral tone for everyone else.

This ethical backbone fortifies the company's legacy against scandals or internal breakdowns.

19.9 Honoring the Human Side of Leadership

A lasting legacy involves how you treat the people under your care:

- **Empathy in Policies**: From family-friendly schedules to mental health support, ensure employees feel valued as human beings.
- **Career Growth Paths**: Offer clear routes for advancement. Mentorship and skill-building show you care about their progress.
- **Fairness in Recognition**: Provide credit where it is due. Avoid favoritism.
- **Listening Culture**: Keep channels open so staff can voice ideas or concerns safely.

Years later, people often remember leaders who genuinely cared about their well-being, not just the bottom line.

19.10 Handling Leadership Transitions Smoothly

Eventually, you or other top leaders might move on. A well-managed transition ensures stability:

1. **Succession Plan**: Identify who can take over key positions and groom them ahead of time.
2. **Gradual Handover**: Give the new leader overlap time to learn roles and build rapport with staff.
3. **Communicate Early**: Let everyone know about the change in leadership structure. Clear communication prevents rumors and anxiety.
4. **Preserve Institutional Memory**: Encourage the departing leader to document key contacts, ongoing projects, and personal insights about the team.
5. **Support the New Leader**: Publicly back them and reinforce their authority. If staff sense you undercut them, morale can drop.

Smooth transitions protect the culture and momentum you have built.

19.11 Leveraging External Networks

A lasting leadership impact often involves relationships outside the company:

- **Industry Connections**: Share your alliances with suppliers, professional associations, or thought leaders so future managers can maintain them.
- **Community Outreach**: If you have engaged in local volunteering or partnerships, ensure the organization knows how to continue these ties.
- **Client Trust**: Introduce your successor or key staff to important clients well before you leave, easing any concerns about service continuity.
- **Media and Public Relations**: If you have built a good reputation, let the next generation know the main media contacts or PR strategies that have worked.

Passing on these external ties strengthens the organization's standing after you step down.

19.12 Creating a Learning Organization

One powerful legacy is a workplace that self-improves over time. Encourage:

1. **Continuous Skill Upgrades**: Provide training budgets, shared reading materials, or internal workshops.
2. **Open Feedback**: Whether it is from employees, clients, or internal reviews, push the habit of learning from mistakes and adjusting quickly.
3. **Knowledge Sharing Events**: Regular short sessions where different teams present findings or tips.
4. **Curiosity Culture**: Reward employees who question standard methods and propose improvements.
5. **Cross-Functional Projects**: Encourage staff from varied departments to collaborate, expanding their understanding of the entire business.

A learning culture adapts and thrives no matter who is at the helm.

19.13 Avoiding Ego-Driven Leadership

Some leaders focus too much on personal accolades, overshadowing the broader mission. This can weaken the foundation they leave behind. Tips to avoid that:

- **Credit the Team**: Publicly highlight the contributions of team members. Resist the urge to center all success on yourself.
- **Share Visibility**: When meeting top executives or media, bring along key staff who actually did the project work.
- **Admit Mistakes**: Show humility if something goes wrong. This builds trust and respect.
- **Encourage Diverse Voices**: Let different people propose solutions. Do not insist on final approval just for the sake of power.
- **Step Back Sometimes**: If you see a capable employee can handle a spotlight moment, let them shine.

Ego-driven bosses might leave short bursts of achievement, but not the robust, enduring impact that a more modest leader can create.

19.14 Balancing Tradition and Innovation

A stable legacy does not mean freezing the company in place. You want to protect core values while allowing future leaders to adapt. Steps:

1. **Document Core Principles**: Specify what is truly non-negotiable, like ethical conduct or respect for employees.
2. **Stay Flexible on Strategy**: The next generation should have room to pivot if markets shift.
3. **Encourage Upgrades**: If older processes become outdated, expect successors to refine them.
4. **Define Legacy Boundaries**: Clarify which parts of the culture or system are crucial to preserve. Let everything else evolve freely.

A balanced approach ensures your foundational work endures without stifling needed growth.

19.15 Mentoring Successors Directly

In some cases, you will have the chance to coach your replacement or the next top-level manager:

- **Regular Check-Ins**: Schedule one-on-one meetings to discuss leadership challenges.
- **Shadowing Opportunities**: Let them watch you handle negotiations, major client talks, or strategic meetings.
- **Detailed Feedback**: After they lead a meeting or a project, debrief them on what went well and what could improve.
- **Share Networking**: Introduce them to your professional contacts, bridging the gap so they can maintain those links.
- **Encourage Their Style**: Do not force them to copy you exactly. They should find their own approach, guided by your advice.

This hands-on mentorship creates continuity and confidence for the incoming leader.

19.16 Measuring the Impact of Your Leadership Legacy

How do you know if you have built something that lasts? Possible indicators:

1. **Employee Retention and Satisfaction**: If staff turnover remains low and people enjoy their work, it is a sign of a healthy environment.
2. **Success After You Leave**: Check how the department or project fares once you are gone. Does it continue thriving or falter?
3. **Continuity of Values**: If employees still use the principles you established to guide decisions, your cultural impact is strong.
4. **Number of Internal Promotions**: If many roles are filled from within, it suggests you successfully grew talent.
5. **Lasting Partnerships**: Clients or partners remain loyal to the organization rather than only to you personally.

Such measures reflect whether your influence truly embedded into the company fabric.

19.17 Handling Resistance to Change

Building a legacy often means updating or restructuring certain areas. Some employees may resist. Tips:

- **Explain the Vision**: Show how the new system or culture benefits them and the broader team.
- **Offer Support**: Provide training or resources for those uneasy about the changes.
- **Involve Them**: If they participate in shaping the new processes, they are more likely to accept.
- **Stay Patient**: Culture shifts do not happen overnight. Steady reinforcement is key.

Over time, results speak for themselves, and skepticism usually fades.

19.18 Facing External Challenges

Your legacy might be tested by market downturns, new competitors, or regulatory hurdles. A robust foundation helps you adapt:

- **Scenario Planning**: As explained before, think through possible external shifts so you are ready.
- **Resilient Culture**: If your team is used to ongoing learning and mutual support, they can pivot faster when external shocks happen.
- **Strong Relationships**: Loyal customers, partners, and staff can help you weather tough conditions.
- **Review and Update**: Keep an eye on which parts of your legacy still hold up and which need refreshing.

Leaders who plan for the outside world create an adaptable, long-lived impact.

19.19 Personal Growth and Reflection

Even as you focus on leaving a lasting mark, do not forget your own development:

- **Seek Feedback**: Ask mentors or colleagues for input on your leadership style.
- **Attend Workshops**: Keep sharpening your skills, whether in strategy, conflict resolution, or public speaking.
- **Self-Awareness**: Recognize your weaknesses and how they might affect the legacy you build.
- **Stay Open to Ideas**: If a junior staff member suggests a new angle, consider it carefully rather than dismissing it.
- **Balance Work and Personal Life**: A stable leader who avoids burnout can devote more energy to guiding others.

Your growth journey continues as you guide others to become leaders in their own right.

19.20 Conclusion of Chapter 19

A legacy of strong leadership is not about chasing glory for a moment but about ensuring the organization flourishes for years, shaped by healthy principles, robust processes, and a pipeline of capable successors. By clarifying values, sharing knowledge, and promoting new leaders, you anchor a vision that withstands turnover or industry shifts. Ethical standards and genuine care for human potential form the base, giving employees and partners a sense of trust that persists. When you eventually step aside, the systems and culture you leave behind continue to guide progress, reflecting the depth and thoughtfulness of your leadership.

In the final chapter, we will explore the future of leadership. With rapid technology changes, evolving workforce demographics, and global challenges, bosses must adapt faster than ever. By looking ahead and preparing your team for tomorrow's demands, you complete the loop—merging time-tested wisdom with forward-facing insights, ensuring that leadership remains effective and relevant in the next era.

Chapter 20: Preparing for the Future of Leadership

The modern workplace is transforming rapidly. Globalization, remote collaboration, automation, and shifting employee expectations all place new demands on leaders. Methods that worked a decade ago may not be enough for tomorrow's challenges. In this concluding chapter, we examine emerging trends, potential disruptions, and how to equip yourself and your team to face an uncertain but opportunity-rich future. By adapting proactively, you keep your leadership relevant, your staff engaged, and your organization competitive.

20.1 Why the Future Demands New Leadership Approaches

1. **Accelerated Change**: Industries can alter dramatically in a short period, meaning leaders must be ready to pivot.
2. **Diverse Workforce**: Global talent pools bring varied cultural norms, communication styles, and skill sets.
3. **Technological Disruption**: Automation and artificial intelligence reshape job roles, requiring leaders to manage transitions.
4. **Rising Employee Expectations**: Younger workers especially value flexibility, purpose, and a healthy work-life balance.
5. **Ecological and Social Pressures**: Environmental concerns and social justice issues also shape customer and employee demands.

Leaders who keep the same old playbook risk falling behind. Openness to learning and experimentation is crucial.

20.2 Embracing Technological Integration

In the future, tech will not just be an add-on; it will be integral to every part of business. Steps:

- **Stay Updated**: Follow industry blogs or tech news to spot relevant innovations early.

- **Evaluate ROI**: Not every new gadget or software suits your needs. Assess the value carefully before adopting.
- **Train Staff**: Provide learning resources so employees can handle upgraded systems confidently.
- **Balance Automation with Human Touch**: Tasks that are repetitive or data-heavy might be automated, freeing people for creative or interpersonal roles.
- **Protect Data and Privacy**: As you integrate advanced tools, keep security measures robust. A data breach can erode trust.

Leaders who navigate technology wisely empower their teams to work smarter, not harder.

20.3 Managing a Hybrid and Flexible Workforce

Remote and hybrid work models are likely here to stay. This shifts how leaders operate:

1. **Clear Remote Policies**: Define expectations for availability, meeting attendance, and communication styles.
2. **Outcome-Focused Management**: Judge employees by results, not hours spent in an office chair.
3. **Cultural Connection**: Find ways to include remote or flexible staff in team events and decision-making, so they do not feel isolated.
4. **Efficient Tools**: Provide platforms for video calls, instant messaging, project tracking, and file sharing that are user-friendly.
5. **Well-Being Checks**: Virtual employees may face loneliness or overwork. Regular personal check-ins matter.

A leader who masters flexible structures can attract a wider talent pool and keep morale high across distance.

20.4 Adapting Skills for a Changing Environment

Future bosses need to expand their skill sets:

- **Data Literacy**: Understanding how to interpret analytics and statistics helps in making better decisions.
- **Cross-Cultural Communication**: Teams might span multiple countries. Sensitivity to language nuances and cultural norms is key.
- **Emotional Intelligence**: As automation handles repetitive tasks, human connection, empathy, and creative thinking become even more valuable.
- **Continuous Learning**: Regularly update your knowledge through online courses, conferences, or reading.
- **Futuristic Thinking**: This includes scenario planning for how technology or market trends might evolve, so you can guide your team with foresight.

By actively improving these abilities, you stay equipped to lead in a complex world.

20.5 Leading Through Complexity and Uncertainty

Leaders must become comfortable making decisions with partial information:

1. **Flexible Goal-Setting**: Identify core objectives but remain ready to pivot if new facts emerge.
2. **Risk Management Tools**: Use scenario planning or stress tests to see how strategies hold up under varied conditions.
3. **Communication**: Be upfront about unknowns; let the team know the reasoning behind each decision, even if it might change later.
4. **Empower Agile Teams**: Encourage smaller groups to react quickly to new challenges, rather than waiting for top-down directives.
5. **Allow Small Failures**: A culture that tolerates controlled failure (and learns from it) can adapt faster to surprises.

Harnessing complexity means not trying to eliminate it but learning to maneuver within it effectively.

20.6 Fostering Inclusion in Global Teams

Workforces are increasingly diverse in terms of culture, gender, ability, and viewpoint. Leaders of the future must ensure everyone feels respected:

- **Language Sensitivity**: Provide translations or use clear, simple English if the group is multinational.
- **Inclusive Policies**: Tackle discrimination or bias promptly. Reward those who promote harmony.
- **Celebrations of Diversity**: Mark special cultural holidays or events in a balanced way—ensuring all staff's backgrounds get acknowledgment.
- **Diverse Role Models**: Showcase leaders from varied backgrounds so employees see a pathway to grow.
- **Ongoing Training**: Regular sessions that discuss unconscious bias or cultural differences can open minds.

Inclusion fosters creativity and loyalty, crucial assets in a competitive market.

20.7 Handling Gig and Contract Workers

Not everyone on your team may be a full-time employee. Freelancers or contract staff are common, bringing unique challenges:

1. **Clear Project Scopes**: Define deliverables, deadlines, and payment terms in writing.
2. **Integration**: Treat gig workers respectfully. Let them access necessary information or tools to do their job well.
3. **Open Communication**: Keep them in the loop about project changes. They will contribute better if fully informed.
4. **Payment Fairness**: Pay promptly according to agreed terms. A good reputation with contractors ensures future talent availability.
5. **Legal Compliance**: Check local labor laws regarding independent contractors vs. employees, so you do not face legal surprises.

By managing this flexible workforce effectively, you can scale up or down quickly while maintaining quality.

20.8 Environmental and Social Responsibility

Modern employees and customers increasingly consider how businesses affect the planet and society:

- **Green Policies**: Reduce waste, recycle, or use renewable energy if feasible. Small changes can add up.
- **Ethical Supply Chains**: Track whether suppliers treat workers fairly and adhere to laws.
- **Community Projects**: Sponsor local programs or encourage employees to volunteer.
- **Transparency**: Publish clear reports on environmental impact and steps for improvement.
- **Integration with Core Strategy**: Make sure these efforts align with business goals; token gestures do not fool informed stakeholders.

Leaders who prioritize sustainability can win trust, retain eco-conscious staff, and meet growing consumer expectations.

20.9 Emphasizing People-Centric Leadership

Automation and AI will take over routine tasks, leaving people-focused leadership more critical than ever:

1. **Coaching and Mentoring**: Freed from micromanaging daily tasks, you can guide employees' growth.
2. **Interpersonal Connection**: The boss who invests time to understand employees' aspirations fosters stronger commitment.
3. **Creative Collaboration**: Humans excel at brainstorming, emotional insight, and nuanced communication—skills that AI cannot replicate well.
4. **Conflict Mediation**: Machines do not handle interpersonal disputes; leaders do.
5. **Visionary Thinking**: Humans can form big-picture strategies that combine empathy, ethics, and reason.

Future success hinges on nurturing the human side of the enterprise, even as technologies evolve.

20.10 Investment in Upskilling and Reskilling

Roles can shift rapidly if certain tasks become obsolete. A forward-thinking boss helps staff adapt:

- **Learning Grants**: Offer subsidies for courses in new software, advanced analytics, or other key skills.
- **In-House Workshops**: Host sessions on emerging topics, taught by internal experts or external trainers.
- **Career Pathways**: Map out how employees can move into evolving positions, so they are not caught off guard.
- **Recognition of Adaptability**: Give credit to those who learn new capabilities or adapt quickly, showing others this is valued.
- **Partner with Institutions**: Some organizations collaborate with universities for specialized programs.

By consistently broadening skill sets, the whole team can pivot nimbly when market demands shift.

20.11 Leading Virtual and Augmented Reality Spaces

Emerging tech like VR (virtual reality) or AR (augmented reality) might change collaboration, training, or product demos:

1. **Pilot Projects**: Experiment with VR-based training simulations for safety drills or advanced skill practice.
2. **Customer Experience**: If applicable, let customers preview products in VR or AR.
3. **Cross-Location Unity**: A shared virtual workspace can make remote staff feel more connected.
4. **Skill Gaps**: Provide tutorials on using these tools, especially if staff are unfamiliar with VR/AR hardware.
5. **Cost-Benefit Analysis**: This tech can be pricey. Ensure it truly solves a need before major investments.

Leaders who take advantage of immersive tech without overhyping it can stand out in certain fields.

20.12 Building Agility into Organizational Structure

In a fast-moving future, rigid hierarchies can be slow. Agile structures distribute power:

- **Small, Autonomous Teams**: Each group handles a project from start to finish, speeding decisions.
- **Rapid Feedback Loops**: Teams release early versions, gather user input, and revise quickly.
- **Transparent Information Flow**: Reduce gatekeeping so staff can access data needed to innovate.
- **Minimal Bureaucracy**: Simplify approval processes. Lean frameworks help you avoid layers of sign-offs.
- **Empowered Staff**: Let employees at all levels propose improvements. Top-down command often hampers nimble changes.

Agile organizations adapt to market surprises faster, essential for future survival.

20.13 Mental Health Support as a Leadership Priority

With constant change, stress levels can rise. Future-focused leaders must consider:

1. **Proactive Monitoring**: Encourage employees to mention stress or burnout signs early.
2. **Professional Resources**: Employee assistance programs, counseling, or wellness webinars can help.
3. **Flexible Policies**: Let staff take mental health days or work from home temporarily if it aids recovery.
4. **Remove Stigma**: Talk openly about mental well-being. A boss who addresses it without shame fosters a safer environment.
5. **Lead by Example**: Balance your own work habits. If you never rest, your team may assume they cannot either.

Supporting mental health can reduce turnover, maintain morale, and enhance overall effectiveness.

20.14 Ethical Use of Data and AI

As data grows, so do privacy concerns and potential biases in AI:

- **Privacy Guidelines**: Only gather the minimum data required. Let users or employees know what is collected and why.
- **Responsible AI**: Monitor algorithms for unfair treatment, such as bias in hiring or performance reviews.
- **Human Oversight**: Important decisions (like promotions or major investments) should not be based solely on machine results without a human check.
- **Compliance with Regulations**: Laws around data use are evolving. Stay up-to-date to avoid legal trouble.
- **Ethical Reviews**: Form committees or designate individuals to review big data or AI projects for potential harms.

Leaders who handle data responsibly build trust and avoid ethical pitfalls.

20.15 Embracing Lifelong Leadership Development

In the past, a boss might settle into a role for years. Today, you must keep evolving:

1. **Personal Reflection**: Periodically evaluate your leadership style. Are you clinging to outdated habits?
2. **Shadow Other Leaders**: Learn from peers, mentors, or even subordinates who excel in certain skills.
3. **New Challenges**: Accept roles or projects that stretch you, from global expansions to cross-department initiatives.
4. **Continuous Education**: Whether it is short online courses or advanced degrees, remain curious.
5. **Feedback Cycles**: Request feedback from staff every few months, then take visible steps to improve.

A dynamic leader never stops refining their approach in response to changing conditions.

20.16 Encouraging Entrepreneurial Thinking

Large companies increasingly value the mindset of quick experimentation and resourcefulness found in startups:

- **Idea Incubation**: Create small "innovation labs" where employees can test bold concepts without heavy red tape.
- **Seed Funding**: Allocate modest budgets for pilot projects. This encourages staff to propose new revenue streams or cost-saving methods.
- **Fail-Friendly Environment**: If a plan does not work out, gather lessons and pivot. Do not punish well-intentioned attempts.
- **Cross-Functional Teams**: Combine marketing, engineering, operations, etc. in small squads that mimic startup dynamics.
- **Reward Initiative**: Recognize those who show creative drive and success in these endeavors.

This approach blends corporate stability with entrepreneurial agility, positioning you well for unexpected shifts.

20.17 Strengthening Global Mindset

More firms serve worldwide customers or collaborate with distant partners. Leadership must evolve:

1. **Cultural Training**: Understand norms for communication, punctuality, or negotiation across regions.
2. **Multiple Time Zones**: Be thoughtful when scheduling global meetings, rotating times so one group is not always inconvenienced.
3. **Local Empowerment**: If you have offices abroad, trust local teams to adapt corporate goals to their market realities.
4. **Language Support**: Provide translations or bilingual staff where necessary.
5. **Global Compliance**: Tax laws, labor regulations, and data rules differ by country, so keep track of changes carefully.

A leader who respects worldwide diversity and local autonomy can thrive in the global arena.

20.18 Navigating Frequent Disruptions and Crises

Pandemics, supply chain breakdowns, or political shifts can unsettle markets quickly. Leaders need resilience:

- **Scenario Exercises**: Routinely simulate disruptions and plan responses.
- **Backup Suppliers**: Relying on a single vendor or region is risky if something major happens there.
- **Financial Buffers**: Maintain emergency funds or flexible credit lines.
- **Adaptive Culture**: Encourage employees to share signals of potential trouble early and propose creative fixes.
- **Communication During Emergencies**: Provide frequent, honest updates. Listen to concerns and show empathy.

By preparing for worst-case scenarios, you minimize panic and act swiftly when surprises strike.

20.19 Encouraging Transparency and Accountability

Future employees and consumers value openness:

1. **Regular Team Updates**: Share progress on major initiatives. If issues arise, communicate them rather than hide them.
2. **Ethics Reporting**: Invite staff to report unethical behavior safely, perhaps via anonymous channels.
3. **Public Transparency**: When relevant, issue statements on company performance or social initiatives, building trust with the public.
4. **Correct Errors Promptly**: If an error or oversight occurs, own up to it and outline steps to fix it.
5. **Build an Honest Reputation**: Over time, consistent honesty forms a brand that can weather controversies better than secretive organizations.

Honesty attracts customers, employees, and partners who appreciate clarity in a complicated world.

20.20 Conclusion of Chapter 20 (and the Book)

As the world continues changing at a rapid pace, leaders cannot afford to remain static. They must adjust to new technologies, evolving workforce preferences, and complex global challenges. Success in tomorrow's landscape calls for flexibility, empathy, cultural awareness, and steady ethics. At the same time, the core principles of good leadership—clear communication, fairness, accountability, and strategic thinking—remain as relevant as ever.

By uniting timeless fundamentals with forward-facing skills, you can guide your organization through shifting conditions and lay the groundwork for ongoing progress. From fostering creative minds to balancing remote and in-person collaboration, from ethical data use to championing diversity and mental health, each aspect prepares your team for an uncertain but opportunity-filled future. In doing so, you not only fulfill your role as a boss today—you also shape a positive work environment that can adapt and flourish for years to come.

Short Version of the Book

Being a great boss involves more than giving orders. It requires guiding people with fairness, clarity, and purpose. Early on, a boss must understand that leadership is about service and ethical responsibility. Trust is central—once established, employees gain confidence to share ideas and collaborate more effectively. Communication should be clear and considerate, ensuring everyone knows what is expected. Setting motivating goals, handling conflict tactfully, and maintaining a healthy workplace culture underpin a stable environment where productivity thrives.

Training and developing the team is key: as people sharpen their abilities, the entire organization becomes stronger. Balancing authority and empathy prevents extremes—employees respect a fair boss who listens. Avoiding common mistakes like micromanagement and ignoring feedback saves time, money, and morale. Leading through change, measuring performance sensibly, and promoting personal accountability keep progress on track. Long-term business relationships, both inside and outside the company, extend support networks and give an advantage over competitors. Recognizing achievements thoughtfully encourages higher engagement without being excessive or superficial.

Handling stress, encouraging creativity, and making sound decisions all push a team toward excellence. By appreciating different personalities, distributing tasks well, and preparing for the future, a boss nurtures a legacy that endures past their own tenure. This includes shaping a culture of learning, growing future leaders, and ensuring robust processes. Finally, adapting leadership approaches to emerging challenges—like remote work, rapid tech advances, and global demands—cements the path for ongoing success. In a changing world, combining proven principles with flexible, forward-thinking methods ensures that the team remains strong, innovative, and ready for what comes next.

www.ingramcontent.com/pod-product-compliance
Lightning Source LLC
LaVergne TN
LVHW012045070526
838202LV00056B/5599